Fee   gination

THE VEGETARIAN SOCIETY COOKBOOK

Compiled by

HEATHER MAIRS

Published by
Sigma Press, 1 South Oak Lane, Wilmslow, Cheshire, SK9 6AR, England.

British Library Cataloguing in Publication Data
A CIP record for this book is available from the British Library.

ISBN: 1-85058-596-2

Typsetting and Design: Sigma Press, Wilmslow, Cheshire.

Cover Design: The Agency, Wilmslow

Illustrations: Jean Brooke-Taylor

Editorial: Ann Giblin

Printed by: MFP Design & Print

Foreword

– from Paul and Linda McCartney

As patrons of The Vegetarian Society and vegetarians for more than twenty years, we are delighted to be associated with the Society's first cookbook. We are convinced that the best way to demolish the myth that vegetarian food is boring and bland is by example. The more people are offered and encouraged to produce varied and tasty vegetarian meals, the more likely they are to appreciate that a vegetarian diet is not about denial and negatives. It is more about being liberated from traditional ideas about diet and taking positive action for yourself and the planet. Indeed, the tremendous variety of fruits, vegetables, nuts, seeds and grains which are now readily available make the choice of meat-eaters seem limited by comparison.

Today, more and more people around the world are becoming aware that what they eat affects their well-being. Increasingly, people are becoming convinced that a move away from meat and meat-based products represents a healthier alternative. But they still want their food to be attractive, interesting and varied. There has been a clear need for vegetarian recipes for food of today. Colourful and exciting food which often has a surprise element – an unexpected ingredient or a twist in the way in which ingredients are combined. These recipes have it all! They represent a contemporary vegetarian way of cooking which is at least as sophisticated as that of the meat-eating tradition. And the great thing about these dishes is, of course, that you can eat them with a clear conscience, confident that nothing has suffered to put your food on the table.

We hope that people who are not vegetarian, perhaps demi-veg or considering the possibility, will be encouraged to dip into these recipes. It may seem a challenge to change your approach to food, but this book should lead you to a more imaginative, enjoyable and rewarding way of cooking. Try these recipes and you'll find that you won't miss meat.

Vegetarians know from experience that leaving out meat does not mean that you have to sacrifice taste, variety or creativity. In fact, many of them become more enthusiastic about food once they begin to experiment. And they do this knowing that it is also the healthiest, more environmentally friendly option, both for themselves and the planet since a plant-based diet requires less water, land and fossil-fuel in its production.

It is fitting that this book, which so clearly demonstrates that vegetarian cooking has grown up, should be published as the Society celebrates its first 150 years. We wish every success to both.

Preface

Too many cooks spoil the broth – but not in this book, as this is the work of many cooks, both professional and amateur. Some dishes have graced the tables of restaurants whilst others have merely been scribbles stuck to the refrigerator. However, the one thing they have in common is that they are dishes that have been created by enthusiasts.

My aim in compiling this book is to share this enthusiasm and make cooking as pleasurable as possible and hopefully eradicate any notion that vegetarian eating is anything but exciting. With recipes such as these, it is in fact tasty, lively and has extreme variety.

When invited to write this book, I couldn't have been happier. I would go as far to say that food is a total addiction for me, especially when accompanied with a glass of good red wine! Considering how central to our lives is the enjoyment of good food, all too many people believe that they haven't got time to cook and that is why the character of this book echoes my philosophy of food – that is, to keep it simple. I feel this appreciation of simplicity in cooking can eventually transform eating habits.

'Feeding the Imagination' offers an inexhaustible choice and variety of dishes, as it is such a wonderfully diverse mix of styles. I really do hope that you enjoy preparing and eating the dishes as much as I did compiling them.

Finally, my deepest thanks to Ann Giblin, my editor at Sigma Leisure, who gave me the most splendid support and guidance. Thank you, Ann – compiling this book would not have been possible without you.

Heather Mairs

Thanks to . . .

I would like to thank the following people for contributing recipes, and offer a very special thank you to the Cordon Vert Cookery School team for both their support and involvement in recipe development and testing.

Cordon Vert Cookery School staff:

Jane Billinge

Lyn Weller

Deb Clark

Rachel Tyldsley

Eddy Hoosan

Rona Acton

Cordon Vert Cookery School graduates:

Kevin Plummer

Julie Phelan

Nunally Patterson

Lynn Brody

Chrys Goote

Gretel McEwan

Michael Lydsey

The Vegetarian Society:

Melanie Wilkinson, Trustee

Kathy Silk, Trustee

Denise Rooke

Joanna Power

And:

Chico Francessco, The Citrus Tree

Michael Pettit, Gardners restaurant, London

Greens Restaurant, Didsbury

The Potato Marketing Board

The Mushroom Bureau

John Nottingham, Kendals, Manchester

Michele Barlow, freelance cookery demonstrator

R. Foster, friend

Betty Wildgoose, my mum

David Hopkins, Plymouth College of Further Education

Contents

Contents

About
Vegetarianism
& Vegetarian Cookery

Why Vegetarian?

People become vegetarian for a variety of reasons. Many believe that it is wrong to slaughter animals for food and object to the suffering that is inflicted upon animals farmed for food. Others choose a vegetarian diet for health reasons. For these people the research into the health benefits of a vegetarian diet is the decisive factor. There are also those who do not eat meat because they are convinced that a plant-based diet is more environmentally friendly. They are swayed by factors such as the reduction in deforestation and lower levels of pollution which would result from a general shift towards vegetarianism. Many people who choose to become vegetarian are influenced by more than one of these considerations.

What is a Vegetarian?

A vegetarian is someone who eats only food which is free from any ingredients obtained from the slaughter of animals. Vegetarians do not eat any meat, poultry, game, fish, shellfish or crustacean, or slaughter by-products, such as gelatine or animal fats.

Vegetarian or Vegan?

- Lacto-ovo-vegetarian – Eats both dairy products and free-range eggs.

- Lacto-vegetarian – Eats dairy products but not eggs.

- Ovo-vegetarian – Eats eggs but not dairy products.

- Vegan – Eats no dairy products, eggs, or any other animal product (including honey).

Many vegetarians who eat eggs will eat only free-range eggs. The Vegetarian Society only endorses products containing eggs if the eggs are certified as free-range.

For vegetarians who eat dairy products, a vegetarian cheese is available that is made from rennet from a microbial source. Cheese is generally made with rennet extracted from the stomach lining of slaughtered calves. The Vegetarian Society only endorses products containing cheese if the cheese is vegetarian.

Checklist of Vegetarian Alternatives

Never suitable	*Alternatives*
Meat, fish, poultry, game	Nuts, seeds, pulses, grains, tofu, tempeh, seitan, TVP, nutmeats
Meat, fish and poultry stocks – in sauces, stock cubes and mixes. There are anchovies in some brands of Worcestershire sauce, for example.	Make vegetable stocks or use vegetarian stock cubes, powders and bouillon.
Animal rennet – used in most cheeses. Whey from animal rennet cheese – used in many processed foodstuffs.	Vegetarian cheese – made with microbial enzymes in place of rennet. Vegetarian margarine – contains no animal rennet whey. Check all labels.
Gelatine or aspic	Agar agar (sea vegetables), gelozone
Animal fats – suet, lard and fish oils. These are often found in manufactured products such as margarine.	Vegetable oils, hardened pure vegetable fat, vegetable oil and butter

Eggs and their by-products (for example, albumen) are sometimes added to manufactured "vegetarian" foods. Check the ingredients list – it should state the source of free-range eggs. Similarly, lactose and casein, which are milk products and so unacceptable to vegans and possibly vegetarians if derived from whey, are used in many different processed foods. The only solution is to check all labels carefully. Alcoholic drinks also often contain animal-derived products. Isinglass is used for fining and cochineal for colour. Vegetarian and vegan wines are available, however. The Society's seedling symbol on any product is the best assurance of its suitability.

Basic Nutrition

As with any diet, variety is the key factor. Eating well doesn't require elaborate meal planning. Having a simple awareness of what we need to eat to keep healthy is all that is required. If a wide range of foods is eaten, a vegetarian diet is no more likely to be lacking nutritionally than any other.

The following is an easy reference guide to help you choose foods that can be combined to create tasty, nutritious meals.

Carbohydrates

Carbohydrates are the body's chief energy source. Most people, vegetarians or meat-eaters, have no problem in obtaining an adequate supply, and any excess is stored as fat.
Good vegetarian sources: pasta, cereals, potatoes, rice, pulses

Fats

While the body does require fats – they provide energy, vitamins A, D, E and K and essential fatty acids – for most people the problem is that their intake far exceeds their requirements. This is why it is important that vegetarians do not replace meat with dairy products only – it is simply swapping one source of animal fat for another. The link between high fat consumption and health problems is now clearly established and generally accepted, so it's obviously a good idea to restrict fat consumption and to particularly avoid saturated fats which are mostly animal fats.
Good vegetarian sources: vegetable oils, avocados, nuts, olive oil, good quality margarine

Fibre

Natural fibre is vital to the healthy functioning of the digestive system. The plant-based diet of a vegetarian will clearly supply an abundance of dietary fibre, but variety is needed to provide the full range of fibre.
Good vegetarian sources: pulses, nuts, wholemeal bread, fruit and vegetables

Protein

The proteins in our food are essential for growth and for the body to function healthily. Proteins are made up of amino acids. Eight of these are described as "essential" because although vital, they cannot be synthesized by the body itself, they have to be provided by our food. Animal proteins provide all of the essential amino acids in the proportions required by the body. No one plant food is able to do this, but all eight essential amino acids are available in a vegetarian diet. Eating a balanced selection of plant proteins in a vegetarian diet will fulfil the protein requirements without overloading the fat content of the diet, and will also provide a good supply of fibre.
Good vegetarian sources: tofu, rice, pulses, lentils, yeast extract, bean sprouts, wholegrains

Vitamins

Although the body requires only tiny amounts of vitamins, they are vital for its healthy functioning. We rely on our food to supply the vitamins. Daily vitamin requirements vary – the young, elderly, pregnant women and convalescents may require a higher daily intake. Requirements are also increased by the Pill, alcohol and smoking. Vegetarians eating a varied diet are unlikely to have a problem fulfilling their daily vitamin requirements. Vegans, children and pregnant or breastfeeding women may wish to increase their B12 intake, but there is also a good range of B12-fortified foods.

Good vegetarian sources of *vitamins:*

Vitamin B group: green leafy vegetables, bananas, yeast extract, mushrooms, peanuts

Vitamin B12: soya milk, fortified cereals, miso, yeast extract, seaweed

Vitamin C: broccoli, citrus fruits, peppers, blackcurrants

Vitamin D: fortified cereals, margarine

Vitamin E: green leafy vegetables, yellow vegetables, Tahini, nuts, seeds, avocados, vegetable oils

Vitamin K: molasses, vegetable oils, green leafy vegetables, seaweed

Minerals

Minerals are also required in minute quantities and must be obtained from food on a daily basis. Smoking, alcohol and taking regular medication affect the body's mineral requirements. A well-nourished vegetarian with a varied diet including plenty of mineral-rich wholefoods and nuts should not have a problem in maintaining a balanced supply of minerals.

Good vegetarian sources of *minerals:*

Calcium: tofu, broccoli, figs, swede, brazil nuts, watercress

Iodine: seaweed, green leafy vegetables

Iron: tofu, pulses, spinach, pumpkin seeds, watercress

Magnesium: soya beans, bananas, cashew nuts, prunes, green leafy vegetables

Zinc: lentils, pumpkin seeds, almonds, oats, sesame seeds

An A – Z of Hidden Animal Products

It is not always easy to be sure that food products are suitable for vegetarians and you may need to check labels carefully. The following list will help you to identify common ingredients which could cause problems for vegetarians or vegans:

Animal fat	Dairy fat is OK for lacto-vegetarians (but not for vegans), carcass-derived fat, e.g. lard or tallow, is suitable for neither. See also **edible fats.**
Aspic	This is a savoury jelly derived from meat or fish.
Beer	All cask-conditioned "real ales" will have been fined (cleared) with **isinglass.** Some keg, bottled and canned bitters, milds, stouts and some lagers may also use isinglass.
Biscuits	Check for animal fats.
Bone	Used in bone china and sometimes for cutlery handles.
Bread	Most large producers use vegetable-based emulsifiers, local bakers may not. Some bakers may grease the tins with animal fat.
Breakfast cereal	Often fortified with **vitamin D3**, derived from lanolin.
Butter	Pure butter is suitable for vegetarians.
Capsules	Usually coated with **gelatine** *(see later)*, though vegetarian alternatives are coming onto the market.
Caviar	Fish eggs. The fish must be killed to obtain the eggs.
Cheese	Likely to have been produced using animal rennet.
Chips	May have been fried in or pre-coated in animal fat.
Chitin	Produced from crab and shrimp shells.
Chocolate	May contain whey *(see later)* and emulsifiers, which may be derived from animal products.

Chymosin	Along with pepsin, a constituent of rennet used in cheese making. Chymosin can also be produced genetically and is identical to that obtained from calf stomach cells.
Cochineal	E120, made from crushed insects.
Crisps	Often use whey or lactose as a flavour-carrier. Salted crisps are the only clearly vegetarian flavour, although some beef crisps are flavoured with yeast extract and are therefore suitable.
E120	*See Cochineal*
Edible fats	Can mean **animal fats**.
Emulsifiers	May not be vegetarian.
Fatty acids	May be of animal or vegetable origin.
Gelatine	A gelling agent derived from animal ligaments, skins, tendons, bones etc.
Glycerine	May be produced from animal fats, synthesised from propylene or from fermentation of sugars.
Gravy	Vegetarian gravy mixes are available. Be careful in restaurants.
Honey	Avoided by vegans.
Ice cream	Look out for non-dairy fats, E numbers, eggs, whey.
Isinglass	A fining agent derived from the swim-bladders of certain tropical fish, especially the Chinese sturgeon. Used in some beers and wines.
Jelly	Usually contains **gelatine**, although alternatives are available.
Lactose	Produced from milk, sometimes as a by-product of the cheese-making process.
Lanolin	Produced from sheep's wool. Used to make **vitamin D3**.
Lecithin	Nearly always produced from soya beans, although it can be produced from eggs.
Margarine	May contain animal fats, vitamin D3, E numbers, whey, gelatine.
Pasta	May contain egg (usually battery) or squid ink.

Pastry	May contain animal fat.
Suet	Usually made from animal fat, but vegetable versions are available.
Sweets	Look out for **gelatine** in boiled sweets and mints.
Vitamin D3	This is obtained from lanolin in sheep's wool; only Vitamin D3 which is guaranteed to be sourced from wool sheared from live sheep is considered acceptable.
Whey	Whey and whey powder are invariably by-products of the cheese-making process which mainly uses animal rennet.
Worcester sauce	Most brands contain anchovies.
Yogurts	Some yogurts contain **gelatine**.

The Vegetarian Kitchen

Many of the recipes in this book rely on distinctive ingredients and flavours. Most of the ingredients are now readily available, but keeping a well-stocked store cupboard will make vegetarian cooking easy and convenient. This list is not intended to be exhaustive, but it would produce a good stock of basics. Less familiar items which are used in the recipes are included to give a guide to their appearance and use – these ingredients are generally available in health food shops.

Grains and Cereals

These are cultivated members of the grass family and form a staple food in many parts of the world. When eaten in large amounts they provide a good source of protein.

Some cereals contain gluten. People suffering from gluten intolerance or coeliac disease need to avoid the following: wheat, rye, barley and oats. Gluten-free ingredients are marked with this symbol: *GF*

Rice *GF*

The numerous varieties of rice that exist are an indication of both regional taste and geographical differences.

- **Short grain rice** has a soft texture and is sticky when cooked so it is suitable for use in puddings.

Above: Grilled Goats Cheese on a Mango Coulis (see page 26)
Below: Tuscan Olive Bread (page 166)
Preceding page: Heather Mairs, compiler of 'Feeding the Imagination'

Port and Stilton Pâté (page 22) - preparation and, below, the finished product.
Overleaf: Roast Vegetable Tarts (page 30)

- The grains of **long grain rice** are dry when cooked and stay separate. It is used in pilaffs and other savoury dishes.

- **Brown (wholegrain) rice** contains substantially more nutrients than white rice. It has a distinctive nutty flavour and a chewy texture. Brown rice should be fresh and carefully stored.

- **Basmati rice** is a superior quality, aromatic rice from India. The taste is superb!

- **Arborio rice** is a round grain Italian rice which has a creamy, moist texture when cooked. In risottos, it gives a really authentic Italian taste.

Wild rice

Wild rice is an aquatic grass, not a rice. It does, however, look like a rice and combines well with long grain rice – which is useful as wild rice is expensive. Its colour is dark and it has a subtle nutty flavour and chewy texture.

Quinoa *GF*

Quinoa, pronounced *keen wah*, has a very high protein content. It has a light taste and texture. There are several varieties, but the white is most common and is considered the best.

Wheat

Bulgar (also known as bulgur) wheat is the traditional ingredient for tabbouleh. The grains have been steamed and cracked. To prepare, soak in boiling water or vegetable stock for 15 minutes. It is a good thickening agent for soups and casseroles.

Couscous is dried, cracked wheat. It is prepared in the same way as bulgar wheat.

Pasta

Pasta is a low fat, high fibre food that combines well with vegetables and sauces. Bought fresh pasta contains eggs which will not usually be free-range. Dried pasta sometimes contains eggs – do check the label.

Pasta has become a staple part of almost everyone's diet, whether vegetarian or not. It is clearly no longer used exclusively in Italian recipes, but incorporated in a wide variety of dishes and served with sauces which reflect the full range of cooking styles and influences. When choosing a pasta shape to use in a recipe, a good rule to follow is that hollow or twisted shapes work well with chunky sauces. The flatter the pasta, the richer the sauce should be.

When cooking pasta, allow 100g/4oz of pasta per person. To prevent the pasta from becoming sticky, always cook in plenty of boiling water, with added salt and a little oil.

Polenta *GF*

Polenta is derived from maize flour and is used in Italian dishes. It can be rather bland so needs strong added flavourings.

Pulses (legumes)

Pulses, or dried peas, beans and lentils, are the dried seeds of pod-bearing plants of the leguminosae. As they have a delicate, non-intrusive flavour, they respond well to the use of herbs, spices and other flavouring ingredients. Pulses are an excellent source of protein, fibre, B vitamins and iron. They are also low in fat – what more could you ask for?

- **Preparation** – Pulses should be soaked before cooking. They need to be soaked in cold water for at least 12 hours then drained and rinsed well. The exceptions to this rule are lentils, split peas, black-eye and mung beans.

- **Cooking** – Pulses need to be cooked correctly as they can be difficult to digest. Cover with plenty of fresh cold water and bring to the boil quickly. They then require simmering without a lid until tender.

- **Kidney beans**, however, should be boiled vigorously for 10 minutes to destroy enzymes that can cause serious stomach upsets.

If pulses are prepared and cooked correctly, there should be no digestive problems. Changing the soaking water several times before cooking and adding a strip of kombu seaweed or a pinch of aniseed to the cooking water also helps.

Canned pulses can be invaluable as a convenient alternative when time is short. It is preferable to choose varieties without added ingredients as so many contain salt and sugar.

Nuts

Nuts are a very concentrated form of food and are high in protein, rich in iron, calcium and zinc. The fat content of nuts is often high, although, apart from coconut, it is mostly unsaturated. It is advisable to purchase nuts in their shell if you wish to keep them in store. They need to be stored in airtight containers and kept in cool conditions as the high fat content allows them to go rancid quickly.

Nuts form the principal ingredient of many vegetarian dishes, including stuffings, roasts, pâtés, croquettes and burgers. Nuts are far more digestible if used ground. Roasting enhances the intensity of flavour of some nuts – hazelnuts and peanuts in particular – but does, however, decrease the nutritional level slightly. Nuts are also excellent to use as a basis for sauces such as nut creams. These are a superb dairy-free alternative.

Soya Products

Many foodstuffs are derived from the soya bean. It is known, quite rightly, as the magic bean.

- **Soya milk** is available in sweetened, unsweetened, and a concentrated form. In addition to soya milk, there is a wide range of flavoured desserts, soya yoghurts and soya creams.

- **Tofu** is also known as soya bean curd. It is available in soft or firm form. Tofu is highly nutritious and cholesterol-free. It has very little flavour of its own, but absorbs flavours really well. Soft tofu, known as silken, is usually used as a blending ingredient in dips, dressings or desserts.

- **Tempeh** is derived from fermented soya beans and has a unique flavour. It has a very different texture from tofu. Again it is a protein rich food which is cholesterol-free. It is used in savoury dishes and is excellent in stir-fries, casseroles and burgers, or skewered onto a kebab.

- **Textured vegetable protein** (TVP) is a high protein food made by extruding vegetable protein in soya beans. To prepare, allow twice its weight of vegetable stock and soak until it has hydrated. As it swells to three or four times its dry weight, it really is an economical ingredient.

- **Miso** is a concentrated paste derived from soya beans and grains (rice or barley). It has a distinctive, salty taste so needs to be used sparingly. The easiest way to use miso is to dilute it with a little water before adding to dishes.

- **Soy sauce** is produced in a similar way, but without the added grains. The only soy sauces worth cooking with are shoyu or tamari. Tamari is gluten-free.

Sea Vegetables

Seaweed is the essential ingredient for Japanese cuisine. It has premium nutritional qualities, comparing favourably to leafy green vegetables. Most seaweed is sold dried and all need soaking before cooking apart from nori. Use in soups, stir-fries, salads, or for wrapping rice balls or sushi.

Cookery Notes

Throughout this book, please note:

- All recipes will serve four people, unless otherwise stated.
- Both metric and imperial measures are given, but follow one or the other – do not mix them.
- All eggs used are free-range size 1.
- Unless otherwise stated, all spoon measures are level.
- All wines and other alcoholic beverages used are vegan.
- All vinegars used are suitable for vegans.
- All cheeses used are vegetarian.
- Vegetarian Parmesan is available from some specialist shops, but can sometimes be difficult to track down. Grana padano is a good alternative and a vegetarian version is imported from Biraghi. If neither of these is available, use a vegetarian pecorino as this has a good strong taste. There is also a soya-based Parmesan available from health food stores which is suitable for vegans. Throughout this book, any of these options will be suitable where a vegetarian Parmesan is required.
- All the pasta used is vegan.
- Information sheets are available from The Vegetarian Society on the above.

Ovens and cooking times do vary – use the times given as a guide, and adjust according to your experience of your oven. Centigrade temperatures should be reduced by 20 degrees if you are using a fan-oven.

Soups and Starters

Tomato and Coconut Soup
vegan

This soup is equally delicious served hot or cold.

3 beef tomatoes or 6 ripe, flavoursome tomatoes
15ml/1tbsp olive oil
1 medium onion, peeled and finely chopped
1 fresh red chilli, de-seeded and finely chopped
900ml/1½ pints tomato and herb stock (use a cube dissolved in boiling water)
5ml/1tsp black mustard seeds
100g/4oz creamed coconut, grated
salt and freshly ground black pepper
20ml/1 heaped tbsp fresh chopped coriander

1. Grill the tomatoes until the skins start to blacken and burst. Peel and chop roughly.

2. Heat the olive oil in a large saucepan and fry the onion and chilli for two minutes. Add the tomatoes, stock and mustard seeds and bring to the boil. Reduce the heat and simmer for twenty minutes.

3. Remove from the heat and stir in the creamed coconut. Allow to cool.

4. Liquidize, season and reheat.

5. Just before serving, sprinkle with coriander and serve with crunchy croutons (optional).

To prepare the croutons, take two slices of bread, remove the crusts, and brush both sides of each slice with a little olive oil mixed with a fresh herb of your choice. Bake in the oven at 200°C, 400°F or Gas Mark 6 for 15 to 20 minutes until crisp. Cut into cubes.

If you like your tomato soup to be very red, stir in 15-30ml/1-2 tablespoons of tomato purée at stage 2.

Pumpkin & Roast Garlic Soup
can be vegan

This colourful soup is excellent for chilly autumn evenings and ideal for
Hallowe'en suppers.

1 head garlic, cloves separated but unpeeled
50g/2oz butter or vegan margarine
2 onions, sliced
1kg/2lbs 4oz pumpkins, peeled and chopped
1 litre/2pts vegetable stock or water
salt and freshly ground black pepper
soured cream and chives to serve: optional

Pre-heat the oven to 200°C, 400°F or Gas Mark 6

1. Place the garlic on a baking tray and roast in the oven for 10
   to 15 minutes until tender. Squeeze out the flesh and set
   aside.

2. Melt the butter or margarine in a large saucepan. Sauté the
   onions, with a sprinkling of salt, over a low to medium heat
   until soft and golden brown.

3. Add the pumpkin flesh and cook for a further 4 or 5 minutes.

4. Now add the stock/water and bring to the boil and simmer
   for 10 minutes. Add the garlic and simmer for another 10 to
   15 minutes or until the pumpkin is tender.

5. Allow the soup to cool slightly then blend until smooth.
   Return to the pan, season and reheat to serve.

6. Garnish with a generous swirl of soured cream and snipped
   chives.

Try to find pumpkins with a deep orange flesh and a green skin.
The flavour will be much stronger and sweeter than the
light-fleshed, orange-skinned varieties.

Baked Avocado with a Walnut and Chilli Sauce
vegan

An exciting combination of flavours - much more appealing than most avocado starters.

2 fleshy red chillies
30ml/2tbsp oil
1/2 onion, chopped
2 cloves garlic, chopped
50g/2oz walnuts, ground
150ml/5fl oz vegetable stock
2.5ml/1/2tsp dried oregano or 5ml/1tsp fresh oregano
2 just ripe avocados
salt and freshly ground black pepper
lime or lemon juice
mixed leaves to serve

Pre-heat the oven to 220°C, 425°F or Gas Mark 7

1. Place the chillies on a baking tin and roast for 15 to 20 minutes until the skins are blackened and blistered. Cool.

2. Heat 15ml/1tbsp of the oil and fry the onion for two minutes over a medium-high heat. Add the garlic and cook until they are both well browned.

3. Place the walnuts, stock, onion, garlic and oregano into a blender. Blend briefly.

4. De-seed and skin the chillies. Add the flesh to the blender and blend until smooth. Season to taste.

5. Halve the avocados and remove the stones. Brush with lime or lemon juice and then with oil and bake for 15 minutes, until warm and tender.

6. Arrange the salad leaves on serving plates. Top with avocado halves filled with warmed walnut sauce.

This is a very rich starter. Follow it with a light main course. The sauce can also be used on pasta.

Roasted Red Pepper and Fennel Soup

vegan

Roasting the peppers really enhances the flavour of this tasty and colourful soup.

4 red peppers
30ml/2tbsp olive oil
1 onion, finely chopped
1 fennel bulb, chopped
2 bay leaves
3 cloves garlic, crushed
10ml/2tsp ground fennel
1 litre/2pts vegetable stock
salt and freshly ground black pepper
a handful of fresh parsley

Pre-heat the oven to 220°C, 425°F or Gas Mark 7

1. Roast the peppers in the hot oven until they are lightly charred. Peel off the skin and discard with the seeds.

2. Heat the oil in a large saucepan and sweat the onion, chopped fennel and bay leaves for a couple of minutes. Add the garlic and ground fennel, cover and cook for a further 10 minutes.

3. Add the roasted peppers and the stock to the pan and bring to the boil. Simmer for 10 minutes.

4. Season as required and allow to cool slightly.

5. Using an electric blender, process the soup until smooth.

6. Reheat to the required temperature, garnish with the chopped parsley and serve.

Sweetcorn Soup
can be vegan

This smooth, golden soup is easy to make quickly from store cupboard
ingredients – ideal for unexpected guests.

2 x 350g/12oz tins sweetcorn, drained
600ml/1pt garlic and herb vegetable stock
50g/2oz butter or vegan margarine
1 small onion, peeled and finely chopped
50g/2oz flour
300ml/10fl oz milk or soya milk
salt and freshly ground black pepper

1. Liquidize one of the cans of sweetcorn mixed with a little
   stock.

2. Melt the butter/margarine in a large saucepan and cook the
   onion gently until soft.

3. Stir in the flour and cook for one minute, stirring all the
   time. Gradually add the milk and the rest of the stock,
   stirring continuously.

4. Add the whole and liquidized sweetcorn kernels and season
   to taste.

5. Bring to the boil, stirring constantly, and simmer for 2 to 3
   minutes. Adjust the seasoning and serve.

Spinach and Aubergine Ramekins

The ease with which these flavoursome ramekins can be prepared and the interesting combination of ingredients make them an excellent choice when guests are expected.

I small aubergine, sliced thinly
Oil to sauté
225g/8oz fresh spinach
225g/8oz ground almonds
50g/2oz ground vegetarian Parmesan cheese
I free-range egg
5ml/I tsp salt
5ml/I tsp freshly ground black pepper
10ml/2tsp mixed Italian herbs
I clove garlic, crushed

Pre-heat the oven to 220°C, 425°F or Gas Mark 7

1. Wash the aubergine slices and sauté in olive oil. Set aside.
2. Mix the remaining ingredients in a bowl.
3. Grease 4 ramekins well and place an aubergine slice in each.
4. Spoon the almond and spinach mixture into the ramekins and pack well.
5. Place the ramekins on a baking sheet and bake for 30 minutes. Serve immediately.

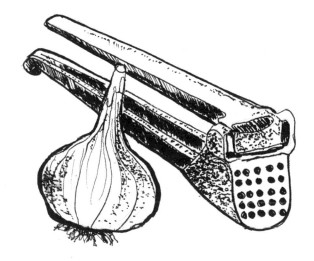

Broccoli, Tarragon and Wine Soup
can be vegan

The wine is the surprise element in this unusual and sophisticated soup –
try it!

60ml/2fl oz olive oil
450g/1lb onions, chopped
2 or 3 cloves garlic, crushed
1kg/2lb 4oz broccoli, chopped finely
450ml/¾ pt white wine
900ml/1½pts garlic and herb vegetable stock
30ml/2tbsp fresh tarragon, chopped
salt and freshly ground black pepper
To garnish – single cream (omit for vegans) and a pinch of paprika.

1. Heat the olive oil in a large pan and sauté the onions and garlic until soft.

2. Add the broccoli, season with salt and pepper and cook gently for 5 to 10 minutes, stirring constantly.

3. Add the wine and stock. Bring to the boil and cook for 5 to 10 minutes, again stirring constantly.

4. Remove from the heat, cool and liquidize.

5. Return to the pan, reheat and add the tarragon.

6. Check seasoning and serve with a swirl of cream (if liked) and a pinch of paprika.

To swirl cream, take a teaspoonful of single cream (do not overload it), touch the tip of the spoon down in the centre of the soup and then lift off a little, quickly swirling it around at the same time.

Mushroom and Olive Pâté
vegan

This is equally good as a tasty snack at any time and any leftovers will quickly disappear.

15g/½oz vegan margarine
75g/3oz closed cup mushrooms, finely chopped
15-30ml/1-2 tbsp red wine
75g/3oz plain tofu
50g/2oz breadcrumbs
5ml/1tsp wholegrain mustard
2.5ml/½tsp dried basil
25g/1oz green olives

1. Heat the margarine in a small saucepan. Add the mushrooms and fry gently for 3 to 4 minutes.

2. Add one tablespoon of the red wine and cook together for a further 3 minutes uncovered. Remove from the heat and allow to cool.

3. Place the mushroom mixture in a food processor along with the other ingredients except the olives. Blend together but do not liquidize. Season to taste and add the rest of the red wine if the pâté is too dry.

4. Chop the olives and stir into the pâté. Refrigerate for at least one hour.

5. Serve, formed into quenelles, with torn watercress, a mild tomato salsa and toast.

Form the quenelles between 2 spoons

Port and Stilton Pâté

A sophisticated pâté which will impress your guests at any time of year, but is an excellent choice for Christmas. It is surprisingly economical to make.

50g/2oz butter
1 bunch spring onions, finely chopped
60ml/2fl oz crusted port*
zest of half a lemon
100g/4oz vegetarian Stilton cheese, crumbled
Small bunch of parsley, finely chopped
freshly ground black pepper

1. Melt the butter in a saucepan and gently sweat the spring onions until soft, add the port and simmer gently for 3 minutes. Remove from the heat.

2. Add the remaining ingredients and stir well.

3. Transfer to a blender and process until the mixture binds together. Check the seasoning.

4. Divide the pâté between individual ramekins and refrigerate for at least 2 hours. Serve with melba toast.

Most port is fined with gelatine, crusted port is always suitable

Drunken Parsnips

This original recipe makes parsnips taste better than you ever
thought they could!

Serves two

Two medium parsnips, cubed
I red onion, chopped coarsely
15ml/I tbsp extra virgin olive oil
I medium orange, juice extracted
90ml/3fl oz port (crusted)
Sprig fresh rosemary
100g/4oz vegetarian Stilton cheese

Pre-heat the oven to 220°C, 425°F or Gas Mark 7

1. Parboil the parsnips for 4 minutes. Drain and place in an ovenproof dish, add the red onion and drizzle with the olive oil.

2. Place in the oven until the parsnips begin to crisp – about 10 minutes.

3. Transfer the parsnips and onion into 2 ramekin dishes, and pour half the orange juice and port into each dish.

4. Return to the oven for about 5 minutes then remove and top with crumbled Stilton and chopped rosemary. Grill until the cheese begins to bubble.

5. Serve immediately with some oat bread to soak up the wonderful juice.

Chargrilled Aubergine Parcels on a Tomato Salsa

This colourful starter is full of the flavours of the Mediterranean. With a simple tomato or green salad it would make an excellent lunch.

2 medium aubergines
I small onion, finely chopped
I clove garlic, crushed
45ml/3tbsp olive oil
I jar tomato passata
15ml/1tbsp fresh basil, torn
15ml/1tbsp fresh oregano
15ml/1tbsp fresh thyme
12 black olives, stoned
15ml/1tbsp fresh chives, finely chopped
425g/15oz ricotta cheese
15ml/1tbsp balsamic vinegar
Salt and freshly ground black pepper
To garnish – a sprig of oregano and a handful of finely chopped parsley

Pre-heat the oven to 180°C, 350°F or Gas Mark 4

1. Cut the aubergines lengthways into quarter inch slices. Salt each slice and leave them in a colander to drain for about 30 minutes while you prepare the salsa.

2. For the salsa, sauté the onion and garlic in olive oil for about 5 minutes. Add the tomato passata and half the basil. Bring to the boil and simmer for 10 minutes, stirring occasionally. Remove from the heat and season to taste. Put to one side.

3. Brush the aubergine slices with a little olive oil and place under a hot grill. Grill for one or two minutes on each side, until they are cooked through. Remove from the heat and stack the aubergines in a dish, sprinkling between the layers with the basil, oregano and thyme. Leave to marinate for half an hour.

4. Meanwhile, prepare the filling for the parcels. Chop 3 of the olives and mix them with the chives and ricotta. Place 2 teaspoons of filling on each aubergine slice and roll up. Place the parcels on a greased baking sheet and heat through in the oven for 10 minutes.

5. Reheat the sauce. Just before serving, stir in the balsamic vinegar.

6. To serve, pour the sauce on individual plates, then add the parcels. Garnish with the oregano and parsley and the remaining olives.

Artichoke Pâté
vegan

Using tinned artichoke hearts is a quick and convenient way to make this light and summery pâté.

425g/15oz tin artichoke hearts
275ml/9fl oz soya yoghurt
handful of fresh parsley
1/4 lemon, juice only
1/2 chilli, de-seeded and finely chopped
a clove of garlic, crushed
salt and freshly ground black pepper

1. Drain the artichokes, and rinse, drain again then place in a food processor.

2. Add all the other ingredients and blend until smooth. Place in a refrigerator for one hour before serving.

3. Serve with warmed pitta bread.

Grilled Goat's Cheese on Mango Coulis

Many different varieties of goat's cheese are now available. Choose a mild flavoured one for this recipe if you haven't tried it before.

6 slices white bread, stamped into rounds
olive oil for brushing
25g/1oz sesame seeds
1 sprig fresh mint, chopped
1 pinch dried chilli flakes
6 x 1cm/½ inch slices goat's cheese
30ml/2tbsp warmed honey

For the coulis:

2 mangoes, peeled and chopped
a dash of white wine

Pre-heat the oven to 220°C, 425°F or Gas Mark 7

1. Brush the bread lightly with oil and bake on a pre-heated baking tray until crisp and golden.

2. Mix together the sesame seeds, mint and chilli flakes. Brush each slice of goat's cheese with honey, then coat the cheese with the sesame seed mixture.

3. Place the cheese on the prepared croutons and bake in the oven until golden brown on the outside and soft inside.

To prepare the coulis:

4. Place the mango flesh in a liquidizer with the white wine and blend until smooth.

5. Spoon a little of the mango coulis on to the base of each plate then top with a goat's cheese-topped crouton.

Porcini Cappuccino
vegan

Cappuccino soups are currently very popular. This one has been developed by Michael Pettett from Gardners restaurant in London. It is deliciously light and frothy and is sure to delight your guests.

15ml/1tbsp olive oil
1 large onion, finely chopped
450g/1lb mushrooms, diced
2 sticks celery, finely chopped
450ml/15fl oz strong vegetable stock
300ml/10fl oz soya milk
a few dried porcini mushrooms, crumbled
freshly ground black pepper

1. Heat the oil in a large saucepan and cook the onion for 2 or 3 minutes. Add the mushrooms and celery and cook gently for 10 minutes.

2. Add the stock and a good grind of black pepper. Bring to the boil and simmer gently for 30 minutes. Add two-thirds of the milk and bring back to the boil.

3. Place in a liquidizer and blend until smooth, then pass through a sieve. Return to the heat.

4. Heat the remaining soya milk and froth in a cafétière by pumping the handle for about 30 seconds.

5. Top the soup with the frothed soya milk and the crumbled porcini.

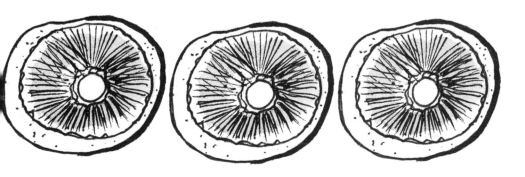

Crumbed Avocado with Lime Tartare Sauce
vegan

The sharp, fresh flavour of lime combines splendidly with the creamy richness of the avocado.

2 avocados – almost ripe
15ml/1 tbsp lemon juice
25g/1oz plain white flour
15ml/1tbsp soya flour mixed with 30ml/2tbsp water
75g/3oz fine white breadcrumbs
vegetable oil and vegan margarine for frying

For the sauce:

90ml/3fl oz soya milk
1 lime, juice and zest
1 clove garlic, crushed
175ml/6fl oz cold-pressed sunflower oil
15ml/1tbsp capers, finely chopped
3 small gherkins, finely chopped
15ml/1tbsp fresh coriander, chopped
salt and freshly ground black pepper
To garnish: a few sprigs of coriander

1. Cut the avocados in half and remove the stone. Peel and slice each half lengthways into 5 or 6 slices.

2. Dip each slice of avocado into the lemon juice, then into the plain white flour and then into the soya flour paste. Finally, coat in breadcrumbs.

3. Heat about 1cm/½inch of vegetable oil and a knob of vegan margarine in a frying pan until the margarine melts and starts to sizzle. Fry the avocado slices for a couple of minutes on each side until golden. Drain on kitchen paper and keep warm.

To make the sauce:

4. Place the soya milk, lime juice, zest and garlic in a blender. Blend briefly. Drizzle the oil through the centre of the lid while continuing to process. Transfer to a bowl and add the capers, gherkins and coriander and season to taste.

5. Serve the warm slices of avocado with some of the sauce drizzled over. Any extra sauce can be served in a jug. Garnish with coriander leaves.

Wild Mushrooms with Cumin
vegan

Wild mushrooms are now widely available and give added texture and flavour when mixed with button mushrooms in this dish.

100g/4oz button mushrooms
100g/4oz wild mushrooms – e.g. shitake or oyster
1 red pepper, roasted, in strips
1 tomato, diced
75ml/5tbsp olive oil
30ml/2tbsp lemon juice
2 cloves garlic, crushed
15ml/1tbsp parsley, chopped finely
a pinch of ground cumin
salt and freshly ground black pepper
8 slices of melba toast

1. Cut the mushrooms to the desired size and place in a bowl. Add the roasted pepper and tomato and combine.

2. Mix together the dressing ingredients and pour over the mushrooms. Leave to marinate for 1 hour before serving.

3. Serve with melba toast.

Roast Vegetable Tarts
vegan

A vegetable rösti is used for the tartlet nests in this delicious recipe.

450g/1lb potatoes, peeled, grated, rinsed and dried
1 large parsnip, peeled and grated
50g/2oz plain flour
45ml/3tbsp vegetable oil
2 peppers, roughly chopped
1 courgette, cut into chunks
2 cloves garlic, crushed
1 red onion, cut into chunks
salt and freshly ground black pepper

Pre-heat the oven to 220°C, 425°F or Gas Mark 7

1. Mix together the grated potato, parsnip and flour. Season with salt and pepper, then bind together with 30ml/2tbsp oil.

2. Place four mounds of the mixture on a well-oiled baking sheet and shape into 10cm/4 inch nests with the edges slightly raised. Cover and chill for 30 minutes.

3. Meanwhile mix together the peppers, courgette, garlic and onion. Toss the vegetables in the remaining oil with salt and pepper, then roast in the oven for 20 minutes.

4. Turn the vegetables over. Uncover the nests and place in the oven on a separate shelf. Continue cooking for about 20 minutes.

5. Transfer the tarts to serving dishes and spoon in the roasted vegetables. Serve immediately.

Crostini

vegan

Originating in Italy, these tiny open sandwiches on a toasted bread base are delicious. Try any combination of savoury ingredients that you fancy for the topping.

60ml/4tbsp olive oil
1 red onion, finely chopped
2 cloves garlic, chopped
75g/3oz sun-dried tomatoes in oil
15ml/1tbsp capers, chopped
75g/3oz black olives, pitted and sliced
1 red pepper, cored, sliced and chopped
5ml/1tsp sherry vinegar
5ml/1tsp sugar
a handful of fresh basil leaves, torn
12 slices French stick, 1cm/½ inch thick
sea salt

Pre-heat the oven to 220°C, 425°F or Gas Mark 7

1. Heat one tablespoon of olive oil in a frying pan and add the onion, fry for 2 to 3 minutes. Add the garlic, tomatoes, capers, olives, pepper, vinegar and sugar and cook over a medium heat for about 5 minutes, stirring occasionally. Stir in the basil leaves, and cook for a further two minutes.

2. Meanwhile, brush the bread with the remaining oil and sprinkle with sea salt. Place the slices on a baking sheet and bake for 5 minutes until crisp and golden.

3. Spread the mixture over the crostini and serve immediately.

Tempura

Tempura is one of the most popular foods in Japan and is considered a special treat. It is bite-sized vegetables dipped into batter and deep-fried.

16 green beans
100g/4oz asparagus tips
1 red pepper, cut into strips
100g/4oz baby sweetcorn
half a cauliflower, broken into florets
100g/4oz button mushrooms
2 carrots, cut into matchsticks
1 banana, peeled and cut into strips
450ml/15fl oz groundnut oil for deep frying

For the batter:

100g/4oz plain white flour
a pinch of salt
2 free-range egg yolks
200ml/7fl oz iced water

For the dipping sauce:

30ml/2tbsp Shoyu
30ml/2tbsp lime juice
5ml/1tsp grated ginger root
1 green chilli, de-seeded and finely chopped
1/4 cucumber, peeled and finely diced
5ml/1tsp sugar

1. To make the batter, sieve the flour with the salt, then lightly beat the egg yolks into the iced water and stir into the flour. Be careful not to over mix – lumps are allowed in this batter!

2. Make the dipping sauce by mixing all of the ingredients together.

3. Heat the oil in a large saucepan. Dip the vegetables in the batter and fry in the hot oil. Several pieces can be fried at one time. Remove with a slotted spoon when crisp and golden and place on absorbent kitchen paper. Keep warm while frying remaining batches of tempura.

4. Serve hot with the dipping sauce.

Stuffed Mushrooms

As well as making an appetising starter to a meal, these mushrooms are wonderful as a buffet dish.

25g/1oz walnuts, chopped
4 large flat mushrooms
1 tbsp olive oil
1 onion, finely chopped
2 cloves garlic, chopped
10ml/2tsp fresh rosemary
50g/2oz couscous
50g/2oz vegetarian Parmesan cheese, grated
30ml/2tbsp sour cream

Pre-heat the oven to 200°C, 400°F or Gas Mark 6

1. Place the walnuts on a baking tray and roast in the oven until golden brown.

2. Remove the stalks from the mushrooms and dice the stems, set aside.

3. Heat the oil in a frying pan and add the onion, cook until transparent. Add the garlic and rosemary and cook gently for 2 to 3 minutes, add the mushroom stalks and season. Stir in the walnuts.

4. Place the couscous in a medium-sized bowl and cover with boiling water, stir and leave to stand.

5. Lower the oven temperature to 180°C, 350°F or Gas Mark 4. Place the mushroom caps on a lightly oiled baking sheet. Mix together the couscous, mushroom mixture, cheese and cream and fill each mushroom cap.

6. Bake the mushrooms uncovered for about 20 minutes. Serve immediately.

Halloumi and Glazed Mango on a bed of Spinach and Coriander

Don't be deterred if you're unfamiliar with some of these ingredients – they are all readily available. This unusual and imaginative combination of flavours and textures looks as exciting as it tastes.

Serves 6

2 packs halloumi, each cut into 6 slices
seasoned flour
olive oil
2 mangoes
15g/½oz butter
10ml/2tsp soft brown sugar
10ml/2tsp kalonji (black onion seeds)
2 cloves garlic, crushed
450g/1lb baby spinach – washed and drained well
half of a small bunch of coriander, chopped
2 limes, juice of
salt and freshly ground black pepper

1. Coat the halloumi slices in seasoned flour. Fry them in olive oil or cook on a griddle pan until golden. Keep warm.

2. Halve the mangoes, peel and cut each half into six slices – see below.

3. Melt the butter and sugar in a frying pan. Add the mango slices and cook for 1 minute over a high heat.

4. Heat 1 tablespoon of olive oil in a saucepan. Add the kalonji and cook for 30 seconds. Add the garlic, spinach and coriander, cook for 2 minutes and season well.

5. Make a mound of spinach on each plate. Arrange the halloumi slices on top. Drizzle lime juice over the cheese and top with mango slices.

6. Serve with rice flavoured with a mango chutney.

You will find it easier to prepare the mango if you imagine the stone in the middle of the mango and cut a piece off either side, as close to the stone as possible.

Pan-Fried Halloumi with Green Olive Dressing on Fresh Herb Leaves

With its refreshing olive dressing and herb salad, this makes a lovely meal for a summer dinner party. It is quick and easy to prepare as long as you remember to cook the halloumi at the very last minute so that it does not become rubbery in texture.

For the dressing:

45ml/3tbsp olive oil
15ml/1tbsp white wine vinegar
5ml/1tsp lemon zest
15ml/1tbsp green olives, drained
5ml/1tsp fresh ground coriander
15ml/1tbsp fresh coriander leaves
1 clove garlic, chopped
5ml/1tsp wholegrain mustard
salt and freshly ground black pepper to taste

To complete:

225g/8oz halloumi
50g/2oz seasoned flour
30ml/2tbsp groundnut/vegetable oil
50g/2oz fresh herb salad

1. Combine the dressing ingredients in a screw top jar.

2. Slice the halloumi into 4 thick slices, and coat in the seasoned flour. Heat the oil in a frying pan and shallow fry on both sides until golden.

3. Arrange the fresh herb leaves on 4 side plates.

4. Place one slice of halloumi on each salad then pour over a generous amount of dressing. Serve immediately.

Feta Samosas

A variation on the usual samosa filling, these tasty treats make a
good buffet dish.

25g/1oz (1 small) courgette, finely grated
100g/4oz feta cheese, crumbled
8 Kalamata (or other black) olives, finely chopped
1 small free-range egg, beaten
2 twists fresh black pepper
5ml/1tsp chopped parsley
25g/1oz unsalted butter
4 9x30cm (3½x12 inches) sheets (yields two triangles per sheet) filo pastry
5ml/1tsp sesame seeds

Pre-heat the oven to 180°C, 350°F or Gas Mark 4

1. Squeeze moisture from the grated courgette.

2. Combine the feta, courgette and olives in a small bowl.

3. Add the egg, pepper and parsley and mix well.

4. Melt the butter and brush one sheet of filo at a time, keeping
the others covered with a slightly damp tea towel. Cut the
sheet of pastry in half and fold each half over lengthwise,
brush with butter again. Place a heaped teaspoon of filling at
the end of the filo strip and fold over to form a triangle.
Continue folding up the triangle.

5. Butter a baking tray and place the filo triangles on the tray.
Brush the tops with butter and sprinkle with sesame seeds.

6. Bake until golden, about 30 to 35 minutes. Serve with a herb
salad.

*Taste the feta cheese before using – if it's necessary, you can
then add herbal salt to the filling.*

Stuffed Baby Courgettes

This is a simple and delicious combination of flavours – wonderful to serve in the summer when courgettes are plentiful.

8 baby courgettes
45ml/3tbsp olive oil
1 onion, finely chopped
1 green chilli, de-seeded and finely chopped
100g/4oz smoked cheese, grated
30ml/2tbsp fresh coriander, chopped
salt and freshly ground black pepper

Pre-heat the oven to 180°C, 350°F or Gas Mark 4

1. Cut the courgettes lengthways, scoop out the flesh and chop. Set aside.

2. Heat 15ml/1tbsp of the oil and fry the onion and chilli for 2 or 3 minutes. Add the courgette flesh and cook gently for a further couple of minutes.

3. Mix together the cheese, coriander and onion mixture and season to taste.

4. Place the courgette boats on a baking sheet and brush them with the remaining oil.

5. Fill each of the courgettes with the mixture and place in the oven. Cook for about 10 minutes, until well browned and bubbling.

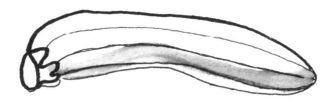

Main Courses and Side Dishes

Pasta with Mushrooms and a Warm Spicy Vinaigrette
can be vegan

The aromatic combination of roast vegetables and warm vinaigrette
complements perfectly the subtle flavours of the mushrooms
– simple but superb.

2 red peppers
2 red chillies
3 cloves garlic, skins on
135ml/9tbsp olive oil and extra for roasting
45ml/3tbsp white wine vinegar
225g/8oz pasta bows
25g/1oz butter or vegan margarine
450g/1lb mixed mushrooms *– e.g. oyster, shitake, button, field – sliced thickly*
150ml/5fl oz white wine
1 bunch fresh basil leaves
salt and freshly ground black pepper

Pre-heat oven to 200°C, 400°F or Gas Mark 6

1. Place the peppers, chillies and garlic in a roasting dish,
    drizzle with olive oil and roast in the pre-heated oven.

2. Take the garlic out when it is tender (after about 15 minutes)
    and remove the skin. Leave the peppers and chillies in the
    oven until they are starting to blacken. At this stage, remove
    them from the oven and place them in a bowl which should
    then be sealed with cling film. When the peppers and
    chillies are cool enough to handle, remove the skins and
    seeds and chop the flesh finely.

3. Whisk 8 tablespoons of olive oil into the vinegar. Cream the
    garlic into the mixture and stir in the peppers and chillies.

4. Cook the pasta in boiling water for 8 to 10 minutes or as
    directed on the packet.

5. While the pasta is cooking, heat the butter and remaining

tablespoon of olive oil in a wide frying pan. Quickly fry the mushrooms on a high heat.

6. Add the dressing and white wine and stir to mix. Season to taste. Stir in about half the basil leaves, roughly torn.

7. Serve on a bed of pasta garnished with extra basil leaves.

Placing the roasted peppers in a sealed bowl (or plastic bag) after cooking helps to loosen the skins, making them easier to peel.

Kohlrabi Dauphinoise

The delicate flavour of the kohlrabi is enhanced by the cream. This also makes a wonderful lunch – eaten with some fresh, crusty bread to mop up the juices.

4 medium-sized kohlrabi
50g/2oz butter
275ml/10fl oz double cream
50g/2oz Gruyère cheese
Salt and freshly ground black pepper

Pre-heat the oven to 180°C, 350°F or Gas Mark 4

1. Remove the outer leaves from the kohlrabi and cut into thin slices. Place in a large pan of boiling, salted water and simmer for 15 minutes. Drain and place in an ovenproof dish.

2. Season and dot with butter, pour the cream over the top and sprinkle with the Gruyère cheese.

3. Place in the oven for 40 minutes or until golden brown and bubbling.

Stuffed Acorn Squash

An innovative way to serve a classic fondue sauce.

4 acorn squash of about the same size
2 cloves garlic, cut in half
12 sage leaves, torn
175g/6oz Gruyère cheese, grated
600ml/1 pint double cream
salt and freshly ground black pepper

Pre-heat the oven to 160°C, 325°F or Gas Mark 3

1. Slice a small amount from the bottom of each squash – so that they stand securely on their own.

2. Now cut off the top of each squash and scoop out the seed.

3. Rub the garlic around the sides of each squash and season liberally. Now add the sage leaves.

4. Sprinkle the cheese in the squash and share the cream between the cups. Add a little more pepper at this stage if required. Place on a baking sheet and cook for 1 hour or until tender.

5. Serve as a fondue and eat by breaking off pieces of the squash flesh and dunking it into the delicious cheesy mixture. Serve with crusty bread and a good white wine.

Bean Provençal
can be vegan

This recipe quickly transforms store cupboard ingredients into a really flavoursome dish.

Serves 2 as a main course (or 4 as a starter)

1 medium onion, peeled and finely chopped
1 garlic clove, crushed
25g/1oz butter or olive oil
175ml/6fl oz dry white wine
5ml/1tsp dried tarragon
1 tin chopped tomatoes (425gms)
30ml/2tbsp tomato purée
1 tin mixed bean salad (410gms)

1. Sauté the onion and garlic in butter until they are soft but not coloured.

2. Add the wine and tarragon and continue cooking until the liquid is reduced by half.

3. Now add the tomatoes and purée and bring to the boil, stirring constantly until the sauce has thickened.

4. Add the drained beans to the sauce, reduce the heat and simmer for 5 minutes, stirring occasionally.

5. Season to taste.

If serving this dish as a main course, serve it hot with new potatoes and vegetables.

Aubergine Kiev with Mango Coulis

A satisfying but light dish – it also looks very impressive.

4 medium-sized aubergines
30ml/2tbsp olive oil
I medium onion, peeled and finely chopped
2 cloves garlic, finely chopped
225g/8oz assorted mushrooms, finely chopped
4 sun-dried tomatoes (in oil), chopped
5ml/I tsp dried thyme or I0ml/2tsp fresh thyme
50g/2oz vegetarian Parmesan cheese, cut into very thin slices
I75g/6oz seasoned flour
2 free-range eggs
I75g/6oz fresh breadcrumbs
a little groundnut or vegetable oil for shallow frying
salt and freshly ground black pepper

For the coulis:

450g/I lb can of mango slices in syrup

Pre-heat the oven to 180°C, 350°F or Gas Mark 4

1. Peel the aubergines and slice in half, lengthways. Scoop out the seeds and flesh from the centre, leaving a shell about 0.5cm/¼ inch thick, then place the peeled aubergine halves in cold water until ready to use. Chop the scooped out flesh and reserve.

2. Heat the olive oil in a frying pan and gently sauté the onion and garlic until softened. Add the chopped mushrooms and aubergine flesh and cook for a further 5 minutes.

3. Add the chopped sun-dried tomatoes and thyme and heat through. Season to taste.

4. Remove the aubergine halves from the water. Fill four of the aubergines with the filling, they need to be fairly full. Place shavings of Parmesan cheese over the filling.

5. Brush the rims of the aubergine halves with a little beaten egg and join the two halves of each aubergine together, keeping all the filling hidden inside. Dip each "whole" aubergine in seasoned flour until thoroughly coated.

6. Carefully dip each aubergine in beaten egg and breadcrumbs. Press the breadcrumbs firmly over the whole aubergine.

7. Heat the groundnut oil in a large, non-stick frying pan and gently fry each aubergine to seal the coating. The kiev needs to be light brown all over.

8. Transfer the kievs to a baking sheet and bake in a moderate oven for 15-20 minutes.

To make the coulis:

9. Place the contents of the can of mango slices into a liquidizer and blend until smooth.

10. Serve the aubergine kievs with the mango coulis and a side salad.

Using baby aubergines this dish would make an excellent starter.

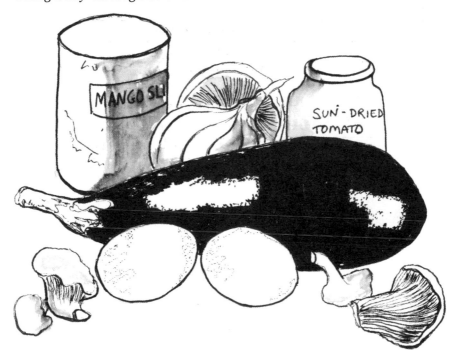

Shallot Tatin with a Walnut and Horseradish Crust
vegan

This is very simple to make, but very satisfying. There is a surprise element in each part which really lifts it out of the ordinary and into something very special.

Serves 6

For the crust:

200g/7oz plain, unbleached flour
a little salt
100g/4oz vegan margarine, cut into 1cm cubes
50g/2oz walnuts, finely chopped or ground
5ml/1tsp vegan horseradish sauce
30ml/2tbsp soya milk
cold water to mix

For the topping:

25g/1oz vegan margarine
15ml/1tbsp olive oil
900g/2lb shallots, peeled (try to use shallots of a uniform size)
45ml/3tbsp muscovado sugar
5ml/1tsp whole cumin seeds
the grated rind of half a lemon or half an orange
30ml/2tbsp balsamic vinegar

Pre-heat the oven to 200°C, 400°F or Gas Mark 6

To make the crust:

1. Lightly grease a 25cm/10 inch, round baking tin. Combine the flour and a pinch of salt in a mixing bowl and rub in the vegan margarine until the mixture resembles coarse breadcrumbs. Stir in the chopped walnuts. If you prefer a finer pastry, use ground walnuts instead of chopped.

2. Mix the horseradish sauce with the soya milk and stir into the flour mixture. Add enough cold water to form a fairly firm dough. Wrap the dough in cling film and put it in the fridge until ready to use.

To make the topping:

3. Heat the vegan margarine and olive oil in a large frying pan and gently sauté the shallots, whole, for 10 minutes until golden brown all over. Keep stirring the pan to prevent the shallots burning.

4. Sprinkle over the sugar, cumin seeds, lemon or orange rind and balsamic vinegar. Add 30-45ml/2-3tbsp water and cook over a slightly higher heat for a further 5 minutes, until the shallots are coated in a thick, syrupy sauce.

5. Place the shallots and sauce over the base of the prepared tin. At this stage another layer of vegetables can be placed on top of the shallots (e.g. lightly sautéed courgette slices).

6. On a floured board, roll the chilled pastry into a circle slightly larger than the baking tin. Place the pastry on top of the shallots, tucking the extra pastry down the sides of the tin. Bake in the pre-heated oven for 20 to 25 minutes, until golden brown.

7. Leave the tatin to rest in the tin for 5 minutes, then place a serving plate over the top and quickly turn the tatin out. Serve warm.

Basil and Mushroom Tarts

Rich and smooth, these tarts are among the best I've tasted and
always popular.

For the pastry:

225g/8oz unbleached white flour
pinch of salt
100g/4oz butter
120ml/4fl oz iced water
1.5ml/¼tsp sugar

For the filling:

25g/1oz butter
225g/8oz chestnut mushrooms, wiped and sliced
1 garlic clove, crushed
15ml/1tbsp white flour
90ml/3fl oz milk
3 spring onions, finely chopped
half a bunch of fresh basil
15ml/1tbsp crème fraiche
salt and freshly ground black pepper

Pre-heat the oven to 220°C, 425°F or Gas Mark 7

To make the pastry:

1. Sieve the flour and salt together. Grate the butter into the
   flour, dipping it into the flour frequently to prevent sticking.

2. Dissolve the sugar in the water and sprinkle over the flour a
   little at a time, cutting the water into the flour to give a firm
   dough. Handle as little as possible.

3. Wrap in cling film and refrigerate for at least 30 minutes.

4. Take out of the fridge and roll into a rectangle, 30 x 12cms
   (12 x 5 inches).

5. Fold the bottom third up and top third down. Turn the pastry through 90° and seal the open edges.

6. Repeat this process three times and then return the pastry to the fridge for 20 minutes.

7. Roll out the pastry and cut out circles to line four 12cm/5 inch, loose-bottom flan tins. Line with greaseproof paper and baking beans.

8. Bake blind for about 15 minutes. Remove the greaseproof paper and baking beans. Glaze the inside and the edges of the flan cases with beaten egg and return to the oven for a further five minutes. Leave on a wire rack to cool until needed.

To make the filling:

9. Melt the butter in a large saucepan and add the sliced mushrooms. Cook for a few moments until just tender.

10. Stir in the crushed garlic and flour. Add the milk slowly, stirring until the mixture boils and thickens.

11. Season to taste. Simmer very gently for about two minutes until the sauce is very thick. Cover the filling with a piece of damp greaseproof paper and place to one side until needed.

12. To finish, place the pastry cases to warm through in a low oven. Stir the spring onions, torn basil and cream into the mushroom filling over a gentle heat and allow to warm through.

13. Fill the tart cases with the mushroom mixture and garnish with a basil leaf.

Cassoulet Castelsarrasin de Famille Albrecht
vegan

This is a French regional dish from the Languedoc district. Ideal for a winter dinner party as the preparation is completed well in advance.

Serves 6 to 8

450g/1lb dried haricot beans (or 2lbs fresh), soaked overnight
4 large onions, finely chopped
1 onion, peeled and studded with 8 whole cloves
6 cloves garlic (smoked garlic if obtainable), chopped
75ml/5tbsp tomato purée
600ml/1pt white wine
2 bay leaves
2 sprigs thyme
2 sprigs parsley
1 celeriac, chopped
1 bulb fennel, chopped
225g/8oz dried chestnuts (soaked in water, then cooked for 30 minutes in fresh water)
grated rind of 1 orange
300ml/10fl oz good quality olive oil

For the topping:

100g/4oz fresh breadcrumbs
50g/2oz chopped parsley
2 cloves garlic, crushed

Pre-heat the oven to 180°C, 350°F or Gas Mark 4

1. Use a very large casserole suitable for the hob and oven, or start the recipe in a large saucepan then transfer it to a very large, ovenproof casserole.

2. Place the beans in the large casserole or saucepan with the chopped onions, the onion studded with cloves, the garlic, tomato purée, half the white wine and the fresh herbs. Add enough water to completely cover the beans.

3. Bring to the boil and boil for 10 minutes. Reduce to a simmer and cook for two hours, until the beans are tender.

4. Remove the studded onion, take out the cloves and discard, chop the onion and return it to the pan. Add the other vegetables, chestnuts, orange rind and remaining wine. Pour over a liberal quantity of olive oil and mix well.

5. Mix the ingredients for the topping together and sprinkle half the amount over the casserole. Bake for 30 minutes.

6. Remove from the oven, break up the topping and stir into the casserole. Sprinkle the remaining topping over and bake for a further 30 minutes.

7. Serve with Braised Red Cabbage with Apple (see following recipe) or a Lollo Rosso and orange salad and crusty bread.

This casserole benefits from long, slow cooking – in rural France it could be cooking for most of the day.

Braised Red Cabbage and Apple
vegan

The best way to serve red cabbage – a wonderful accompaniment to vegetarian hotpots and casseroles.

15ml/1tbsp olive oil
1 onion, sliced
15ml/1tbsp brown sugar
1 medium-sized red cabbage, shredded finely
2 apples, cored and sliced finely
15ml/1tbsp white wine vinegar
150ml/5fl oz red wine
Salt and freshly ground black pepper

Pre-heat the oven to 180°C, 350°F or Gas Mark 4

1. Heat the oil in a large saucepan and sauté the onion until transparent. Add the sugar and stir until the sugar caramelises.

2. Next add the cabbage, apple and vinegar and stir. Add the wine and seasoning.

3. Transfer to an ovenproof dish with a lid, and place in the oven for about 40 minutes.

Farfalle with a Spicy Orange and Lemon Sauce

This unusual pasta dish will quickly become a firm favourite – apart from its distinctive fresh taste, it really does take just minutes to prepare.

225g/8oz farfalle (pasta bows)
15ml/1 tbsp tahini
15ml/1 tbsp tamari
10ml/2tsp sugar
15ml/1 tbsp cider vinegar
10ml/2tsp lemon juice
30ml/2tbsp orange juice
rind of one orange, grated
rind of one lemon, grated
30ml/2tbsp olive oil
3 garlic cloves, crushed
1 vegetable stock cube
10ml/2tsp chilli oil
1 red chilli, de-seeded and finely sliced
2 bunches spring onions, chopped
4 fresh basil leaves
50g/2oz pecorino, grated

1. Cook the pasta in boiling water for 8 to 10 minutes or as directed on the packet.

2. Mix the tahini, tamari, sugar, cider vinegar, lemon juice, orange juice and the grated rind of the orange and lemon in a bowl.

3. Heat the olive oil in a wok then gently sauté the garlic. Add the cooked pasta, sprinkle with the vegetable stock cube and reduce the heat.

4. Add the sauce ingredients along with the chilli oil and toss carefully.

5. Now add the chilli, spring onions, basil and pecorino and stir.

Chestnut Bourguignonne Pie
can be vegan

A hearty, wintery casserole, enclosed in a golden crust, this pie makes a
good centrepiece to serve at Christmas or for the family
on a cold, snowy day!

100g/4oz dried chestnuts, soaked for 6 to 8 hours
2 bay leaves
1 sprig of rosemary or 5ml/1tsp dried rosemary
200ml/7fl oz red wine
300ml/10fl oz vegetable stock or water
25g/1oz butter or vegan margarine
8 small pickling onions or shallots, peeled
100g/4oz chestnut mushrooms, wiped
50g/2oz button mushrooms, wiped
10ml/2tsp Dijon mustard
30-45ml/2-3tbsp tamari or soy sauce
freshly ground black pepper
fresh parsley, finely chopped
225g/8oz vegan puff pastry, thawed if frozen

Pre-heat the oven to 200°C, 400°F or Gas Mark 6

1. Place the soaked chestnuts, herbs and 150ml/5fl oz of wine in a saucepan. Add vegetable stock to cover then cook until just tender – approximately 50 to 60 minutes.

2. Drain the chestnuts, reserving the liquid.

3. Melt the butter in a frying pan and sauté the onions until lightly browned.

4. Add the mushrooms and cook for a further 4 or 5 minutes.

5. Add the chestnuts, the remaining red wine and sufficient chestnut cooking liqueur to cover.

6. Bring to the boil and simmer for 20 to 30 minutes to reduce the liquid a little.

7. Stir in the mustard, tamari and black pepper to taste. Cook for a further 5 minutes.

8. Check the seasoning and consistency and adjust as necessary.

9. Spoon the mixture into a medium-sized pie dish. Roll out the pastry on a floured surface and place on top of the filling.

10. Bake for about 20 minutes, until the crust is golden.

Goan Cream Curry

This recipe is simplicity itself to prepare, but has a subtly smooth yet exotic flavour which you would expect to take far longer to achieve.

60ml/2fl oz groundnut oil
200g/7oz paneer cheese, cubed
5ml/1 tsp salt
10ml/2tsp garam masala
10ml/2tsp ground coriander
5ml/1tsp ground cumin
5ml/1 tsp turmeric
2cm/1 inch root ginger, grated
2 fresh chillies
2 cloves garlic, crushed
120ml/4fl oz water
200g/7oz peas
200g/7oz mushrooms
100g/4oz spinach
120ml/4fl oz coconut milk
120ml/4fl oz double cream

1. Heat the oil in a frying pan and shallow fry the paneer.

2. Add the salt, garam masala, coriander, cumin, turmeric ginger, chillies and garlic and sauté lightly.

3. Add the water and bring to the boil.

4. Add the peas and mushrooms, simmer for 10 minutes.

5. Add the spinach, coconut milk and cream, simmer for 5 minutes.

6. Serve with rice.

Topig: Spicy Chickpeas
vegan

Topig is technically an Armenian dish though I have come across variations
on this throughout the Middle East. These beans are very popular
throughout this region and lend themselves to absorbing flavours very well.

30ml/2tbsp groundnut oil
I large onion, chopped
5ml/I tsp cumin seeds
5ml/I tsp Lebanese masala
5ml/I tsp ground cumin
2 green cardamom pods
10ml/2tsp ground coriander
2.5ml/½ tsp turmeric
450ml/15fl oz water
400g/14oz cooked chick peas
120ml/4fl oz tomato pulp
5ml/I tsp dried mint
2 cloves garlic, finely chopped
small amounts of salt, sugar and lemon juice

1. Heat the oil in a thick-based saucepan.
2. Add the onion and allow to brown.
3. Reduce the heat, add the cumin seeds and allow to fry for
   approximately 1 minute.
4. Add the Lebanese masala, ground cumin, cardamom, ground
   coriander and turmeric, and *lightly* fry.
5. Pour on the water and bring to the boil.
6. Add the chick peas and reduce the heat, simmer for 15
   minutes.
7. After this time, add the tomato pulp, mint and garlic, and
   salt, sugar and lemon juice according to taste. Allow to
   simmer for a further 2 or 3 minutes.
8. Serve with rice or cracked wheat.

*If you are unable to obtain a ready-made Lebanese masala, try
making your own. You will need 5ml/1tsp of each of the following
– black peppercorns, coriander seeds, cumin seeds and whole
cloves, plus 2 green cardamom pods, a pinch of nutmeg, 1cm/½
inch stick cinnamon, 2.5ml/½ tsp chilli powder, 5ml/1tsp
paprika, 2.5ml/½ tsp sumac. Grind all the ingredients together
and keep in a screw-top jar.*

Tomato and Rice Croquettes

These are an excellent accompaniment to any spicy dish.

450ml/15fl oz hot water
50g/2oz tomato purée
5ml/1tsp freshly ground black pepper
10ml/2tsp dried oregano
175g/6oz short grain Italian rice
1 small free-range egg
50g/2oz grated Parmesan cheese
5ml/1tsp salt
sunflower or groundnut oil for shallow frying

1. Bring the water to the boil.

2. Add the tomato purée, black pepper and oregano and mix together.

3. Now add the rice, stir, cover and allow this to cook (about 15 to 20 minutes).

4. Once cooked, add the egg, cheese and salt.

5. Create small croquettes from the rice and allow to cool.

6. Heat a little oil in a frying pan and shallow fry the croquettes until golden brown.

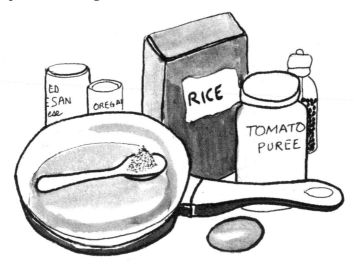

Kizartmasi: Fried Onion, Spinach, Carrot and Potato in Spicy Batter
vegan

Fritters, pakoras, tempura or Kizartmasi – call them what you will – deep-fried vegetables encased in batter are popular worldwide.

225g/8oz gram flour
1.5ml/¼tsp salt
1tsp ground cumin
1.5ml/¼tsp chilli powder
1 medium-sized onion, sliced into half moons
1 medium-sized potato, finely chopped
1 medium-sized carrot, finely chopped
10 spinach leaves, torn coarsely
groundnut oil for frying

1. Sift the gram flour, salt and all the spices into a mixing bowl.

2. Add sufficient cold water to make a light batter that represents a pancake mixture consistency.

3. Now add all the cut vegetables to the batter and mix.

4. Heat the oil in a frying pan.

5. Using a metal spoon, scoop a dessertspoonful of the vegetable and batter mixture into the hot oil.

6. Fry for approximately two minutes on each side until a deep golden brown. Drain on kitchen paper and serve.

Vegetable Jambalaya
vegan

This Creole dish is traditionally quite hot, but this modified version is less spicy. The vegetables can be varied to suit whatever you have available.

50ml/2fl oz olive oil
100g/4oz Tofu
1 large onion, chopped
2 bay leaves
100g/4oz short grain rice
5ml/1tsp salt
5ml/1 level tsp turmeric powder
10ml/2tsp tomato purée
600ml/1pt hot water
1 medium carrot
50g/2oz green beans
4 mushrooms
50g/2oz sweetcorn
1 large sweet potato

1. Heat the olive oil in a pan.

2. Sauté the tofu, remove with a slotted spoon and set aside.

3. Return the pan to the heat and add the chopped onion and bay leaves, and sauté until starting to colour.

4. Add the rice, salt, turmeric and tomato purée and mix together.

5. Pour on the water and allow to come to the boil.

6. Add all the cut vegetables and the tofu, cover and cook on a low heat until the rice and vegetables are cooked and most of the liquid has been absorbed (about 20 minutes).

Sweet and Sour Vegetable Parcels
can be vegan

Filo pastry always makes an interesting 'package' and the sweet and sour
filling in these parcels is sure to please.

30ml/2tbsp olive oil
2 heads of celery, chopped
1 red pepper, diced
1 green pepper, diced
100g/4oz mushrooms, sliced
100g/4oz frozen sweetcorn
100g/4oz frozen peas
1 chilli, chopped
3 cloves garlic, crushed
10ml/2tsp grated fresh ginger
15ml/1tbsp tamari soy sauce
white wine vinegar to taste
120ml/4fl oz orange juice
15ml/1tbsp maple syrup
30ml/2tbsp tomato purée
15ml/1tbsp cornflour
100g/4oz tinned haricot beans, drained
1 packet filo pastry
olive oil or melted butter for pastry

Pre-heat the oven to 200°C, 400°F or Gas Mark 6

1. Heat the oil and fry the vegetables until tender. Begin with
   the fresh vegetables and add the frozen vegetables a little
   later.

2. Add the chilli, garlic and ginger and stir.

3. Now add the soy sauce, vinegar, orange juice, maple syrup
   and tomato purée. Mix thoroughly then thicken with the
   cornflour.

4. Add the tinned haricot beans and heat the mixture through.

5. Leave the mixture to cool.

6. Cut the filo pastry into rectangles 15cm/6 inches by 10cm/4 inches. Take 3 pieces at a time, taking care to keep the remainder covered with a damp cloth. Brush one piece with olive oil or melted butter, place another piece on top and repeat. Place 2 tablespoons of the filling onto one half of the pastry, fold over and seal the edges.

7. Place on a baking tray and brush with olive oil or butter. Bake in the oven for about 10 to 15 minutes, until golden.

Grated cheddar cheese can be sprinkled on the top of the mixture before the parcel is assembled. Omit for vegans.

Sweet and Savoury Mushroom Salad

To create a more exotic tasting dish, try adding a selection of wild mushrooms.

90ml/6tbsp grapeseed oil
45ml/3tbsp red wine vinegar
450g/1 1b button mushrooms
175g/6oz vegetarian Gloucester cheese, cubed
200g/7oz mixed herb leaves
50g/2oz pine nuts, toasted
2 apples, cored and sliced

1. Whisk the grapeseed oil and vinegar in a bowl and pour over the mushrooms. Cover and leave to stand for 2 hours.

2. Stir in the remaining ingredients and toss lightly together. Check seasoning. Serve immediately.

Courgette and Feta Cakes with a Herby Salsa

Feta cheese has become (deservedly) very popular. If you don't like its salty taste, try using crumbled Cheshire cheese in its place – the texture is similar but the flavour is milder.

For the cakes:

450g/1lb courgettes, grated
2 free-range eggs, beaten
100g/4oz feta cheese, crumbled
5ml/1tsp fresh mint, chopped
25g/1oz plain flour
freshly ground black pepper
olive oil to fry

For the salsa:

225g/8oz ripe tomatoes, chopped
50g/2oz red onion, finely chopped
15ml/1tbsp fresh chives, chopped
15ml/1tbsp coriander, chopped
1 lime, juice of
salt & freshly ground black pepper

1. Grate the courgettes and mix with a generous sprinkling of salt. Leave to drain in a colander for 30 minutes. Press out as much moisture as possible.

2. Mix together the courgettes, eggs, feta, mint, flour and lots of freshly ground black pepper.

3. In a frying pan, preferably non-stick, heat 2 tablespoons of olive oil and fry tablespoons of the mixture until golden on one side. Flip them over and brown the other side.

4. Cook the cakes in batches and keep the cooked ones warm in a moderate oven. Add more oil to the pan as necessary.

5. Mix together the salsa ingredients and season.

Take the time to ensure that as much moisture as possible is pressed out of the courgettes. It will make life a lot easier!

Asparagus, Avocado and Blue Cheese Puffs

An unusual combination of flavours in these golden puffs will delight your family and friends. They make an excellent buffet dish as well.

Serves 4 to 6

25g/1oz butter
25g/1oz plain white flour
300ml/10fl oz milk (approx)
1 large, ripe avocado
100g/4oz blue Stilton or Dolcelatte cheese
350g/12oz fresh asparagus, cooked and chopped, or the same weight of tinned asparagus, drained and chopped
30ml/2tbsp fresh coriander, chopped
salt and freshly ground black pepper
450g/1lb ready-made puff pastry (thawed if frozen)
1 free-range egg, beaten
sesame seeds

Pre-heat the oven to 200°C, 400°F or Gas Mark 6

1. Make the sauce – melt the butter in a saucepan, add the flour and cook for 2 minutes on a gentle heat, stirring all the time. Take off the heat and gradually add enough milk to make a thick sauce – stirring after each addition. Return to the heat, bring to the boil then simmer, stirring all the time, for 5 minutes.

2. Mash the avocado and cheese together then stir into the sauce with the chopped asparagus and coriander. Season to taste and leave to cool.

3. Roll out the pastry thinly and cut into twelve 12.5cm (5 inch) squares. Put equal quantities of the mixture on the centre of each square. Moisten the edges and fold over to make a triangle. Brush with beaten egg and sprinkle with sesame seeds.

4. Place on a greased baking sheet and bake for 15 to 20 minutes until puffed up and golden.

As a change from steaming fresh asparagus, try brushing with oil and grilling until it starts to colour – this gives added flavour.

Tagliatelle with Cashew and Coconut Sauce
vegan

The exotic flavours of Thailand have influenced this sauce, with the classic combination of lemon grass, chilli, coriander and coconut. Tossed with pasta this is a real taste sensation!

1 root fresh lemon grass, chopped
1 clove garlic, crushed
1 bunch fresh coriander, chopped
1-2 red chillies, de-seeded and finely chopped
30ml/2tbsp water
2.5ml/½ tsp black peppercorns
225g/8oz tagliatelle
30ml/2tbsp groundnut oil
1 onion, peeled and finely chopped
300ml/10fl oz coconut milk
15ml/1tbsp lemon juice
50g/2oz cashew nuts, toasted
salt and freshly ground black pepper to taste
basil and coriander leaves to garnish

1. In a blender or pestle and mortar, make a paste with the lemon grass, garlic, coriander, chillies, water and black peppercorns.

2. Cook the tagliatelle in boiling water for 8 to 10 minutes or as directed on the packet.

3. Meanwhile, heat the oil in a frying pan and fry the onion for 2 to 3 minutes, until soft. Add the paste and cook on a gentle heat for 2 minutes. Add the coconut milk, bring to the boil and boil fast for 5 minutes, stirring all the time to reduce and thicken the sauce. Stir in the lemon juice.

4. Mix the toasted cashew nuts into the sauce and heat through. Check the seasoning then toss the tagliatelle in the sauce.

5. Serve garnished with basil and coriander and with a crisp side salad.

Szechuan Aubergines
vegan

Szechuan peppercorns (or Fagara) from China, together with chilli, ginger and garlic, give the aubergines an exotic oriental flavour not to be missed.

10ml/2tsp Szechuan peppercorns
4-6 hot, dried chillies
30ml/2tbsp canned flageolet beans, mashed
groundnut oil
675g/1 ½lbs aubergines, chopped
5 cloves garlic, chopped
2cm/1inch grated root ginger, juice of
4 spring onions, chopped
30ml/2tbsp rice vinegar
30ml/2tbsp dry sherry
15ml/1tbsp caster sugar
30ml/2tbsp shoyu
90ml/6tbsp water

1. Dry fry the peppercorns in a heavy pan and grind. Pass through a sieve.

2. Grind the chillies and add to the beans along with the ground peppercorns. Mix well.

3. Heat enough oil in a wok to deep-fry the aubergines in batches until golden brown.

4. Pour away most of the oil, leaving approximately 2 tablespoons. Add the garlic, ginger juice and spring onions, stir.

5. Add the chilli and pepper bean paste. Stir.

6. Now add the vinegar, sherry, sugar, shoyu and water. Cook over a high heat for 2 to 3 minutes and it will be ready to serve.

Each batch of aubergines will soak up most of the oil. Add more oil – most of it will be released before the dish is completely cooked. Serve with rice or couscous.

Sweet Root Vegetable Cannelloni with Parsnip Sauce
can be vegan

A delicious variation on the baked pasta theme.

Serves 6

1 onion, chopped
450g/1lb pumpkin, peeled and chopped
1 sweet potato, peeled and chopped
6 cloves garlic, peeled and left whole
10 sprigs fresh thyme
10 sage leaves
olive oil
175g/6oz parsnips, peeled and chopped
750ml/25fl oz milk/soya milk
grated nutmeg
50g/2oz butter/vegan margarine
50g/2oz plain flour
225g/8oz tinned chestnuts, chopped
18 cannelloni tubes (cooked, if necessary, according to the packet instructions)
salt and freshly ground black pepper
fresh herbs to garnish

Pre-heat the oven to 220°C, 425°F or Gas Mark 7

1. Place the onion, pumpkin, sweet potato, garlic and herbs in a roasting tin. Season and drizzle with olive oil. Roast for 50 minutes or until tender. Remove the thyme sprigs.

2. Cook the parsnips in 150ml/5fl oz of the milk until tender. Purée and flavour with nutmeg.

3. Melt the butter or margarine in a medium saucepan. Add the flour and cook for 1 or 2 minutes, stirring.

4. Remove from the heat and gradually add the rest of the milk,

stirring all the time. Return to the heat and bring to the boil, stirring constantly. Simmer for 2 minutes. Add the parsnip purée and chopped chestnuts and season.

5. Stir 150ml/5fl oz of the sauce into the roast vegetables and use this to stuff the cannelloni.

6. Arrange the tubes in an ovenproof dish and cover with the remaining sauce. Bake for 25 minutes. Garnish with fresh herbs and serve.

Try to buy sweet potatoes with orange flesh which will add colour and flavour to the dish.

Baked Beetroot with Dill Aioli
vegan

An unusual way of serving beetroot, but it is really delicious. Be adventurous with the sauce and vary the herbs – try parsley or capers.

4 medium-sized beetroots, scrubbed but not peeled
90ml/3fl oz soya milk
half a lemon, juice and zest
1 clove garlic, crushed
180ml/6fl oz sunflower oil
10ml/2tsp fresh dill, chopped

Pre-heat the oven to 160°C, 325°F or Gas Mark 3

1. Place the beetroots on a baking tray and cook slowly for about 3 hours, until tender.

2. Remove the beetroot from the oven and peel. Serve them whole or sliced.

3. To make the mayonnaise, place the soya milk, lemon juice and zest and garlic in a liquidizer and blend briefly.

4. Gradually drizzle in the oil while blending, until the mayonnaise emulsifies. Stir in the dill and serve with the beetroot.

Cabbage and Potato Cakes with Red Onion Marmalade
can be vegan

Upmarket 'bubble and squeak' with a delicious accompaniment, this recipe is wonderfully savoury. When cooked in ring moulds and served topped with the marmalade it becomes a fashionable dinner party main course.

3 baking potatoes (no less than 550g/1 1/4lb)
15g/1/2oz butter or vegan margarine
45ml/3tbsp olive oil
2 red onions, sliced
4 medium ripe tomatoes, chopped
2 cloves garlic, crushed
50ml/2fl oz balsamic vinegar
25ml/1 1/2tbsp muscovado sugar
100g/4oz cabbage, chopped or shredded
100g/4oz Brussels sprouts, halved
10ml/2tsp mustard seeds
1 onion, chopped
salt and freshly ground black pepper

1. Bake the potatoes until they are tender. Cool, peel and break up the flesh. Season well.

2. Make the marmalade by heating the butter or margarine and 1 tablespoon of the olive oil. Add the red onions, cover and cook gently for 5 to 10 minutes, until soft.

3. Add the tomatoes, garlic, vinegar, sugar and seasoning. Simmer, covered, for 10 minutes. Remove the lid and simmer for a further 15 minutes. Add a little water if it begins to dry out.

4. Boil the cabbage and sprouts until tender (about 3 minutes). Drain and chop.

5. Heat 1 tablespoon of the oil and cook the mustard seeds for 20 seconds. Add the onion and fry until soft and golden. Finally, add the cabbage and sprouts and cook over a high heat until tinged with brown. Season.

6. Oil four 8 to 10cm/3 to 4inch ring moulds and press potato into the bottom of each one to fill the mould to just under half way. Add a layer of cabbage mixture and top with more potato to fill the moulds.

7. Heat 1 tablespoon of the oil in a non-stick pan and fry the cakes (in the moulds) until the bottoms are golden. Flip them over and brown the other side.

8. Remove from the moulds, arrange on a serving plate and top with the marmalade.

If you have no ring moulds, use small baked bean cans with the top and bottom removed.

Aubergine and Courgette Parmigiana

A simple, tasty and satisfying meal.

2 aubergines, sliced
30ml/2tbsp olive oil
3 courgettes, sliced
425ml/15fl oz tomato sauce (see the next recipe)
30ml/2tbsp freshly chopped basil and oregano
175g/6oz mozzarella cheese, sliced
45ml/3tbsp freshly grated Parmesan cheese

Pre-heat the oven to 200°C, 400°F or Gas Mark 6

1. Place the aubergine slices in a colander and sprinkle with salt. Leave to stand for 30 minutes.

2. Rinse the aubergines and pat dry on kitchen paper.

3. Heat some of the olive oil in a large frying pan and fry the aubergines slices a few at a time until golden brown. Remove from the pan with a slotted spoon and leave on one side.

4. Using the remaining olive oil, fry the courgettes until golden brown. Remove from the pan and reserve.

5. Pour half the tomato sauce in the base of an ovenproof dish then layer with the aubergines, courgettes and herbs. Finish with a layer of the sauce.

6. Cover with the mozzarella cheese and sprinkle with the Parmesan cheese.

7. Bake in the pre-heated oven for about 30 minutes, until the topping is golden brown.

Tomato Sauce
vegan

This basic recipe may be used whenever you need a tomato sauce. For the parmigiana, you will need to double the quantities.

Serves 6

15ml/1 tbsp olive oil
1 small onion, peeled and finely chopped
1 or 2 cloves garlic, crushed
a pinch of chilli powder
225g/8oz fresh plum tomatoes, skinned and chopped
10ml/2tsp tomato purée
a pinch of sugar
15ml/1 tbsp fresh oregano, chopped
15ml/1 tbsp fresh basil, chopped
salt and freshly ground black pepper

1. Heat the oil and fry the onion and garlic until soft.

2. Add the chilli powder, tomatoes and tomato purée, partially cover the pan and simmer for 30 minutes.

3. Season to taste, add the sugar and fresh herbs and stir.

The sauce can be made in advance and then reheated gently just before serving.

Grilled Aubergine, Pepper and Courgette Salad
can be vegan

We tend to think of salads involving raw ingredients, but grilled vegetables with a herby vinaigrette dressing also make a wonderful salad accompaniment to a meal.

Serves 6

1 large aubergine, diced
1 each of red, green and yellow peppers, sliced
2 red onions, each cut into 8 pieces
2 medium courgettes, diced
15ml/1tbsp balsamic vinegar
225g/8oz cherry tomatoes, halved
6 sun-dried tomatoes in oil, sliced
100g/4oz feta cheese, diced (optional)
olive oil for drizzling
sprigs of fresh mint to garnish

For the dressing:

45ml/3tbsp white wine vinegar
2 cloves garlic, crushed
120ml/8tbsp lemon-flavoured olive oil
30ml/2tbsp fresh mint, chopped
30ml/2tbsp fresh chives, chopped
salt and freshly ground black pepper

1. Make up the dressing by mixing all the ingredients together.

2. Mix the aubergines, peppers, onions and courgettes together in a bowl and toss in the dressing. Drain and reserve the dressing.

3. Grill the vegetables, turning frequently, until they start to char. Drizzle extra olive oil over the vegetables if necessary.

4. Mix the balsamic vinegar into the reserved dressing and pour over the cooked vegetables. Allow to cool.

5. Mix the cherry tomatoes, sun-dried tomatoes and feta cheese (if using) into the cooked vegetables. Check the seasoning and transfer to a serving dish.

6. Garnish with mint sprigs.

If you can't find lemon-flavoured olive oil, flavour your own by mixing the finely-chopped zest of 1 or 2 lemons with the olive oil.

Lemon Dhal
vegan

This recipe originates from Bangalore, is very simple to prepare and full of flavour.

50ml/2fl oz groundnut oil
1 large onion, chopped
10ml/2tsp cumin seeds
5ml/1tsp salt
15ml/1tbsp turmeric
2 fresh chillies, chopped
2 cloves garlic
250g/9oz cooked red split lentils
15ml/1tbsp dried mint
the juice of 2 limes
the juice of 1 lemon

1. Heat the oil in a pan and add the onion, sauté until brown.

2. Add the cumin seeds, salt, turmeric, chilli and garlic and sauté for 2 minutes, being careful not to burn the vegetables.

3. Now add the lentils and mint and simmer for 5 minutes.

4. Add the lime and lemon juices and check the seasoning. Serve with plain boiled rice or naan bread.

Avocado, Mango and Orange Salad with Spicy Citrus Vinaigrette
can be vegan

A fruity salad with a tangy, refreshing vinaigrette
– excellent to accompany a summer meal.

2 large ripe avocados, peeled and sliced
2 large oranges, segmented
1 mango, peeled and sliced
¼ to ½ cucumber, sliced
½ Webb's lettuce, shredded
¼ bunch watercress, washed

For the dressing:

15ml/1tbsp runny honey or maple syrup
15ml/1tbsp each of orange, lime and lemon juice
15ml/1tbsp fresh ginger juice
45-75ml/3-5tbsp olive oil
1/2-1 red chilli, de-seeded and very finely chopped
1 clove garlic, crushed
10ml/2tsp red onion, finely chopped
15ml/1tbsp fresh coriander, finely chopped
salt and freshly ground black pepper

1. Make the dressing – mix all the ingredients together in a jar and shake well.

2. Prepare the fruit and salad vegetables. Arrange the shredded lettuce on a large platter or in a shallow, wide bowl.

3. Mix the dressing with the other ingredients and serve on the bed of lettuce, garnished with sprigs of watercress.

Make fresh ginger juice by grating a piece of root ginger and squeezing the juice out of the flesh.

Hot and Sour Noodles
vegan

Traditional Chinese flavours in this stir-fried dish make it popular all year round. Make sure you have all your ingredients prepared before you start to stir-fry as the cooking time is very short.

1pkt Chinese noodles
60ml/4tbsp soy sauce
45ml/3tbsp sweet rice vinegar
45ml/3tbsp vegan sherry vinegar
15ml/1tbsp vegetable oil
10ml/2tsp sugar
30ml/2tbsp sesame oil
2 cloves garlic, crushed
1 chilli, de-seeded and chopped finely
10ml/2tsp fresh ginger, grated
1 red onion, sliced
2 carrots, sliced into matchsticks
2 courgettes, sliced into matchsticks
handful of parsley, finely chopped
50g/2oz peanuts

1. Cook the noodles in a large pan of boiling water for about 4 minutes, drain and rinse under cold water, drain again and set aside.

2. In a medium-sized bowl, combine the soy sauce, vinegars, vegetable oil and sugar, stir and set aside.

3. Heat the sesame oil in a wok, add the garlic, chilli and ginger and fry for 1 minute. Now add the onion and stir, add the carrots and cook for a further couple of minutes, then add the courgettes. Stir-fry for 2 or 3 minutes then remove from the heat.

4. Add the noodles and parsley and toss together. Transfer to a serving dish and sprinkle with the peanuts. Serve immediately.

Roasted Vegetable Lasagne
vegan

Roasted vegetables have become very popular and make an interesting variation on the humble vegetarian lasagne recipe. An innovative twist to this recipe is the use of roasted, creamed garlic in the béchamel sauce – delicious!

Serves 6

450g/1lb cherry tomatoes
1 large onion, peeled and cut into medium chunks
2 courgettes, cut into 2cm/1inch wedges
1 green pepper, cut into 2cm/1inch pieces
1 yellow pepper, cut into 2cm/1inch pieces
6 cloves garlic, peeled and left whole
45ml/3tbsp olive oil
30ml/2tbsp vegan pesto
30ml/2tbsp fresh basil leaves
salt and freshly ground black pepper
225g/8oz lasagne sheets

For the vegan béchamel sauce:

50g/2oz vegan margarine
50g/2oz plain flour
600ml/20fl oz soya milk
yeast flakes, to taste
10ml/2tsp miso
30ml/2tbsp Parmesano (vegan Parmesan)

Pre-heat the oven to 220°C, 425°F or Gas Mark 7

1. Oil the base of a large roasting tin and add all the prepared vegetables and the garlic cloves. Mix the pesto with the remaining olive oil and pour over the vegetables.

2. Roast in the oven for 30 minutes, until the vegetables are tinged brown at the edges. Remove from the oven and reduce the temperature to 200°C, 400°F or Gas Mark 6. Sprinkle the torn basil leaves over the vegetables, season and set aside.

3. Remove the garlic cloves and crush, ready to go in the sauce.

To make the béchamel sauce:

4. Melt the margarine in a saucepan, stir in the flour and cook gently for 2 minutes. Remove the pan from the heat and gradually add all but 30ml/2tbsp of the soya milk, mix until the sauce is smooth.

5. Return to the heat and stir constantly until the sauce thickens. Remove from the heat and season with salt and pepper.

6. Add enough yeast flakes to taste. Mix the miso to a smooth paste with 30ml/2tbsp of soya milk and add to the sauce. Stir in the cooked, crushed garlic and set the sauce on one side.

7. Oil a 20cm x 25cm (8ins x 10ins) ovenproof dish. Place a third of the roasted vegetables in the base of the dish. Place a third of the lasagne sheets in a layer over the top. Cover with a third of the sauce. Repeat the process twice more so you end up with a layer of béchamel sauce on the top.

8. Sprinkle with the Parmesano cheese and bake in the oven for 30 to 40 minutes, until golden and bubbling.

Mini Galettes

These are excellent when served with the subsequent recipe for Red and
Yellow Pepper Sauces.

For the pancakes:

225ml/8fl oz milk
1 free-range egg
5ml/1tsp vegetable oil
75g/3oz plain white flour
pinch salt
oil for frying

For the herb crust:

50g/2oz butter
50g/2oz pine nuts, finely ground
45ml/3tbsp fresh oregano, finely chopped
45ml/3tbsp fresh flat-leaf parsley, finely chopped
Salt and freshly ground black pepper

For the galette filling:

175g/6oz button mushrooms, thickly sliced
1 clove garlic, crushed
90ml/6tbsp olive oil
1 medium aubergine
3 medium onions, sliced into rings

Pre-heat the oven to 190°C, 375°F or Gas Mark 5 – after you have made the
pancakes

To make the pancakes:

1. In a liquidizer mix together the milk, egg and oil. Add the
   flour and salt, blend and leave to stand for at least 30
   minutes. (Alternatively, whisk all the ingredients together in
   a bowl.)

2. Heat 5ml/1tsp of oil in a non-stick frying pan. Place a 8cm/3
   inch round metal pastry cutter in the bottom of the pan.

When the oil has just reached smoking point, place about 15ml/1tbsp of batter mixture in the pastry cutter. Allow to cook for about 30 seconds.

3. Remove the pastry cutter and flip the pancake over. Cook until golden brown.

4. Repeat this process until you have 16 pancakes. Keep the pancakes stacked on a plate with greaseproof paper in between each pancake. Once cooled, refrigerate until needed.

To make the herb crust:

5. In a saucepan, soften the butter over a low heat. Remove from the heat, add the remaining ingredients and mix well. Set aside.

To make the galette filling:

6. Fry the mushrooms and garlic in 30ml/2tbsp olive oil until they are cooked. Set aside.

7. Thinly slice the aubergine and fry in 30ml/2tbsp oil until they are golden brown. (If you prefer, you can de-gorge the aubergine first.)

8. Fry the onions in the remaining oil until caramelised. Drain and set aside.

To assemble:

9. Place 4 pancakes on a greased baking sheet, arrange 3 slices of aubergine on each then top with another pancake. Layer the onion and mushroom in the same way, ending with a pancake. Spread the herb crust on top of each galette.

10. Place in the oven and bake for about 15minutes.

To de-gorge the aubergine, cut into the slices required, place in a colander and salt each layer. Leave over a bowl for 30 minutes to drain off the liquid. Rinse well and pat dry on kitchen paper.

Red and Yellow Pepper Sauces
can be vegan

These simple sauces are very colourful and are an easy way to lift an
ordinary dish.

2 red peppers
2 yellow peppers
25g/1oz butter or vegan margarine

1. Quarter and de-seed the peppers. Place the red peppers in a
   blender and liquidize.

2. Place in a sieve lined with muslin and set over a bowl. Leave
   to one side.

3. Repeat the process with the yellow peppers.

4. In separate saucepans, simmer each pepper liquid until it
   has reduced to a fairly thick, spooning consistency.

5. Add half the butter/vegan margarine to each sauce and
   season to taste.

*Serve a galette with the two sauces on each plate, and have
summer baby vegetables to accompany.*

Spicy Noodles - page 111
Roast Vegetables Torte - page 107

Chestnut Bourguignonne Pie - page 54
Fattoush - page 118

Sweet and Savoury Mushroom Salad - page 61 (The Mushroom Bureau) ;
Asparagus and Baby Sweetcorn Pithiviers - page 114

Mulled Pasta
vegan

An ideal recipe for when you need a filling family meal but time is short. The vegetables can be varied - their flavours will be enhanced by the topping of almonds, cinnamon and sugar.

400g/14oz pasta
extra virgin olive oil
1 head broccoli
100g/4oz green beans
2 leeks, sliced
900g/2lb tomatoes, chopped
2 cloves garlic, chopped
15ml/1tbsp tomato purée, diluted in 30ml/2tbsp water
100g/4oz breadcrumbs
50g/2oz ground almonds
2 cinnamon sticks, ground
15ml/1tbsp brown sugar

Pre-heat the oven to 200°C, 400°F or Gas Mark 6

1. Cook the pasta, drain and place in an ovenproof dish. Set to one side.

2. Heat the olive oil in a large frying pan and fry the vegetables for 3 to 4 minutes.

3. Add the tomatoes and garlic and stir until the tomatoes begin to liquidize. Add the tomato purée mixture and stir. Simmer very gently for 2 to 3 minutes.

4. Remove from the heat and pour over the cooked pasta. Sprinkle with the breadcrumbs, almonds, cinnamon and sugar.

5. Place in the oven and remove when golden.

Mushroom and Spinach Mélange with Citron Couscous
vegan

Flavouring the couscous transforms it from an ordinary grain
accompaniment to a central part in this tasty dish.

225g/8oz couscous
2 lemons, rind of both and juice of one
30ml/2tbsp toasted sesame oil
2 cloves garlic, peeled and chopped
2cm/1inch fresh ginger, peeled and chopped
1 medium red onion, peeled and sliced
225g/8oz mixed mushrooms, (chestnut, oyster, shitake) sliced
225g/8oz fresh spinach, stalks removed and torn
15ml/1tbsp soy sauce
30ml/2tbsp fresh coriander, roughly chopped
25g/1oz vegan margarine
25g/1oz pine nuts

1. Place the couscous in a large bowl with the juice and rind of one lemon. Pour over 600ml/20fl oz of boiling water and set on one side, stirring occasionally.

2. Heat the sesame oil to a medium heat and stir-fry the garlic, ginger and onion for 1 minute.

3. Add the mushrooms and cook for 2 minutes. Add the spinach, remaining lemon rind, and soy sauce, and cook very briefly, until the spinach has just wilted.

4. Remove the wok from the heat, stir in the coriander and season to taste.

5. Drain any remaining water from the couscous. Heat the margarine in a saucepan and quickly fry the pine nuts until golden. Add the couscous and seasoning. Mix well until heated through.

6. To serve, place the couscous on a plate and place the mushroom mixture next to it. Alternatively, place the couscous in a small mould, invert on a serving plate and arrange the mushroom mélange around the sides.

Spinach and Chilli Pastries

Savoury puff pastry pockets with a spicy bite make an interesting main dish.

15ml/1tbsp olive oil
1 onion, chopped
2 cloves of garlic, chopped
red chilli, de-seeded and chopped
225g/8oz fresh young spinach, leaves left whole
1 small lime, juice of
200g/7oz low-fat soft cheese
salt and freshly ground black pepper
225g/8oz puff pastry
milk to glaze

Pre-heat the oven to 220°C, 425°F or Gas Mark 7

1. Heat the oil in a large frying pan. Add the onion with a sprinkling of salt and cook until tender.

2. Add the garlic and chilli and cook for a further two minutes.

3. Now add the spinach and lime juice. Cook for 2 or 3 minutes, until the spinach has wilted.

4. Add the soft cheese, mix thoroughly and season well. Allow to cool.

5. Roll out the pastry and cut out 4 squares 12cm x 12cm/5ins x 5ins. Place a quarter of the filling onto one half of each square. Fold the pastry over to form triangles. Seal the edges.

6. Place on a baking tray. Glaze with a little milk and bake until golden – about 20 to 25 minutes.

Nest of Roasted Balsamic Vegetables with Aromatic Wild Rice
vegan

Another way of using versatile filo pastry is shown in this dish – wonderful for a special dinner party. The marinade of balsamic vinegar, oil and herbs gives the vegetables an interesting flavour.

I packet of filo pastry
45ml/3tbsp sunflower oil
250g/9oz wild rice
I bouquet garni sachet
I small pumpkin, peeled and finely sliced
I large courgette, diced
50g/2oz button mushrooms, diced
I red pepper, diced
100g/4oz French beans, steamed
I small radicchio
30ml/2tbsp balsamic vinegar
75ml/5tbsp olive oil
2 large sprigs of rosemary
I bunch parsley, chopped
salt and freshly ground black pepper

Pre-heat the oven to 180°C, 350°F or Gas Mark 4

1. Place a 10cm/4 inch wide flan ring upside down on a baking sheet. Lightly grease the outside of the flan ring.

2. Brush five sheets of pastry with sunflower oil and place over the flan ring in layers at different angles, resulting in a star shape. Place in the oven for about 10 minutes or until golden brown. Leave to cool for 5 minutes, then carefully lift the nests off the rings and place upturned on a dinner plate. This needs to be done three more times, until you have four baskets. At this stage, raise the temperature of the oven to 200°C, 400°F or Gas Mark 6.

3. Wash the rice thoroughly. Add to a large pan of water with the bouquet garni and bring to the boil. Simmer on a low

heat for 40 to 45 minutes, until the grains have split and are tender.

4. Meanwhile, place all the vegetables in a large bowl and mix. Blend together the balsamic vinegar, olive oil, seasoning and 1 sprig of rosemary. Pour over the vegetables and set aside for 30 minutes for the vegetables to marinate.

5. Grease a large roasting tray and spread the vegetables evenly over the tray. Cover with foil and place in the oven for 15 minutes. Remove the foil and roast for a further 15 minutes.

6. To serve, fill each filo nest with the roasted vegetables and marinating juices. Add the wild rice around the edge of the basket and garnish with the parsley and rosemary.

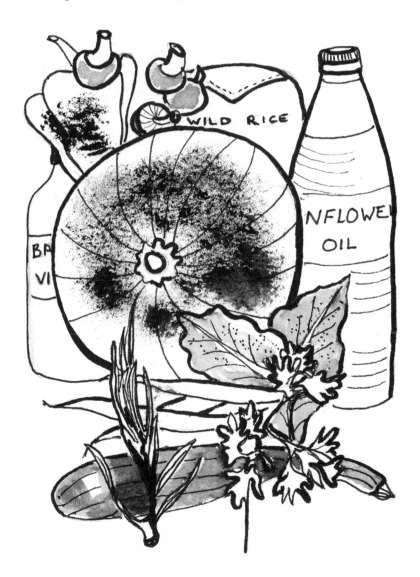

Stuffed Aubergine
can be vegan

The combination of aubergines, mushrooms and cashews is rich but delicious.

Serves 2

1 medium aubergine, cut lengthways
25g/1oz butter or olive oil
1 onion, finely chopped
6 mushrooms, sliced
150ml/5fl oz vegetable stock
1 garlic clove, crushed
15ml/1tbsp tomato paste
50g/2oz cashew nuts, ground
4 sun-dried tomatoes, chopped

Pre-heat the oven to 200°C, 400°F or Gas Mark 6

1. Scoop out the flesh from the aubergine, leaving the skins intact.
2. Cut the aubergine flesh into small pieces.
3. Arrange the skins in a lightly-greased ovenproof dish and cook in the oven for 15 minutes.
4. Heat the butter or oil and cook the onions until they are golden.
5. Add the aubergine flesh and sauté until it softens.
6. Next add the mushrooms and sauté.
7. Add the stock, garlic and tomato paste, then stir and cook for 1 minute.
8. Add the nuts and stir until the stuffing has a creamy texture.
9. Season and mix in the sun-dried tomatoes.
10. Place the filling in the cooked aubergine skin and cook in the oven for 20 minutes.
11. Serve with rice or bulgar wheat.

Fresh Pineapple and Banana Curry
can be vegan

A mild, creamy curry - add more chillies if you prefer it hotter.
Serve with basmati rice and some naan bread.

50g/2oz ghee or oil
spices – grind together in a pestle and mortar:
4 green cardamom pods
2.5ml/½tsp cumin seeds
2.5ml/½tsp ground turmeric
3 whole cloves
5ml/1tsp ground coriander
2.5ml/½tsp fennel seeds
2.5cm/1 inch piece cinnamon stick, chopped
2.5cm/1 inch piece root ginger, peeled and chopped
1 onion, finely chopped
3 cloves garlic, chopped
1 small chilli, de-seeded and chopped finely
1 handful fresh coriander, chopped
1 packet passata (sieved tomatoes)
90ml/3fl oz white wine
½ packet creamed coconut, broken into pieces
150ml/5fl oz single cream or soya cream
1 fresh pineapple, peeled and cut into quartered slices
3 bananas, sliced
425g/15oz tin of chickpeas
3 medium potatoes, cooked and cubed

1. Heat the ghee in a large saucepan and add the spices. Cook for 1 minute, then add the onion and fry for a further couple of minutes. Add the garlic, chilli and fresh coriander and stir. Cook for 2 minutes.

2. Add the tomatoes, wine and creamed coconut and bring to the boil, reduce to a simmer and cover the pan. Cook gently for 10 to 15 minutes, adding water if it becomes too thick.

3. Add the cream, pineapple, bananas and chickpeas and stir. Simmer for a further 5 minutes.

4. Stir in the cooked potatoes and serve hot, garnished with the coriander leaves.

Artichoke, Aubergine and Red Pepper in White Wine and Mushroom Sauce
vegan

Red and black wild rice mixed together make a colourful accompaniment to this rich and tasty dish

200g/7oz wild red rice
50g/2oz wild black rice
I small aubergine, cubed
400g/14oz tin artichoke hearts, drained and quartered
I red pepper, de-seeded and chopped
2 red onions, each cut into 8 pieces
8 garlic cloves, peeled and left whole
60ml/4tbsp olive oil
5-10ml/1-2tsp dried oregano
salt and freshly ground black pepper to taste

For the sauce:

50g/2oz vegan margarine
I small onion, peeled and finely chopped
225g/8oz mushrooms, chopped
25g/1oz plain white flour
300-450ml/10-15fl oz white wine
To garnish: 25g/1oz toasted pine kernels

Pre-heat the oven to 200°C, 400°F or Gas Mark 6

1. Cook the red and black rice together in a saucepan of boiling water for about 40 minutes.

2. Place all the vegetables on a baking tray, season with salt, pepper and oregano and drizzle with olive oil. Bake until starting to char (about 30 minutes).

To make the sauce:

3. Melt the margarine gently in a saucepan, add the onion and cook until soft.

4. Add the mushrooms, cover with a lid and cook for 5 minutes.

5. At this stage add the flour and cook, stirring all the time, for 2 minutes. Gradually add the white wine and bring to the boil, stirring constantly. Simmer for about 5 minutes until thickened. Blend and season to taste.

6. Serve the roast vegetables on a bed of red and black wild rice and pour the sauce over the top. Garnish with toasted pine kernels.

Savoury Summer Pudding
vegan

A variation on a classic English dessert, traditionally made in mid-summer.
If made correctly, there should be no trace of white bread.

extra virgin olive oil
1 red onion, chopped
3 cloves garlic, chopped
handful of fresh basil leaves, torn
1.35kg/3lb tomatoes, peeled and cut in half
30ml/2tbsp red wine
12 to15 slices firm white bread, crusts removed
salt and freshly ground black pepper
bunch of watercress to garnish

1. Heat the oil in a small pan and add the onion, garlic seasoning and basil. Cook until the onion becomes transparent. Remove from the heat and place on one side.

2. In a liquidizer, blend the tomatoes with the red wine then season to taste.

3. Cut the bread into wedges, saving 2 slices, and dip into the tomato mixture.

4. Line a medium-sized pudding dish with the bread. Spoon in the tomato mixture and cover with the slices of bread. Push them down so that the pudding is firm.

5. Place in the refrigerator for about 6 hours. To serve, turn the pudding out onto a serving plate and garnish with watercress.

Artichoke, Green Bean and Pine Nut Risotto
can be vegan

The availability of canned artichokes makes this delicious risotto simple to prepare.

1.2 litres/2pts vegetable stock
100g/4oz fine green beans
30ml/2tbsp olive oil
1 onion, diced
2 cloves garlic, crushed
350g/12oz arborio rice
200ml/¼ bottle dry white wine
5ml/1tsp dried oregano
75g/3oz pine nut kernels, toasted
400g/14oz canned artichoke hearts, drained and quartered
handful flat-leafed parsley, roughly chopped
handful fresh basil, torn
100g/4oz vegetarian Parmesan cheese, optional
salt and freshly ground black pepper

1. Heat the stock to a bare simmer and keep simmering over a very low heat.
2. Bring a pan of water to the boil and add the green beans for 3 minutes. Remove from the water and drain, set aside.
3. In a large frying pan, heat the olive oil and add the onion. Cook for 2 minutes then add the garlic and sauté for a couple of minutes.
4. Add the rice and cook for a further 2 minutes, stirring constantly. Begin adding the stock a ladle at a time, allowing the rice to absorb all the stock before adding more. Continue stirring.
5. When half the stock has been used, add the wine and oregano, stirring constantly. Continue adding the remaining stock, total cooking time will be about 20 minutes. When the last ladle of stock has been added, add the beans, pine nuts, artichoke hearts and herbs.
6. Cook for an additional few minutes, the rice should be al dente, with a bit of bite in the centre.
7. When cooked, remove the pan from the heat, stir in the Parmesan if using and season to taste. Serve immediately.

Hotpot
vegan

A winter hotpot is always welcoming on a cold night. Serve with plenty of greens and season with lots of pepper.

75g/3oz plain flour
75g/3oz self-raising flour
75g/3oz vegan margarine, cut into small pieces
75g/3oz dried soya chunks
30ml/2tbsp bulgar wheat
10ml/2tsp yeast extract
900g/2lb potatoes, parboiled and cut into small pieces
450g/1lb sweet potato, parboiled and cut into small pieces
1 large onion, sliced and sautéed in oil
salt and freshly ground black pepper

Pre-heat the oven to 200°C, 400°F or Gas Mark 6

1. Sieve the flour and a pinch of salt into a bowl, add the pieces of margarine and, using your fingertips, combine the mixture until it resembles breadcrumbs. Add 45ml/3tbsp cold water and combine to form a dough. Chill for 20 minutes in the fridge.

2. Place the soya chunks, bulgar wheat and yeast extract in a bowl and cover with boiling water, stirring until the yeast extract is dissolved. Leave to stand for 5 minutes then drain, reserving the liquid.

3. In a large bowl combine the potatoes, sweet potatoes, onion and soya milk. Season to taste then transfer to a casserole dish, adding some of the reserved liquid (about 150ml/5fl oz).

4. Roll out the pastry to cover the dish, wet the edge of the dish with water and place the pastry over the filling. Press the edge to seal and cut a small hole in the centre. Brush the pastry with milk or egg wash.

5. Bake in the oven for 30 to 40 minutes until the pastry is golden brown.

Provençal Gougère

Choux pastry is so simple to make; with this pastry ring, you could add any filling of your choice.

For the filling:

30ml/2tbsp olive oil
2 red onions, chopped
3 leeks, sliced
2 cloves garlic
45ml/3tbsp white wine
I packet sun-dried tomatoes
30ml/2tbsp mascarpone cheese
fresh basil leaves, torn

For the choux pastry ring:

50g/2oz butter
150ml/5fl oz cold water
65g/2½oz strong plain flour
50g/2oz Gruyère cheese
5ml/1tsp whole grain mustard
a handful of fresh parsley, finely chopped
2 free-range eggs, beaten
salt and freshly ground black pepper

Pre-heat the oven to 200°C, 400°F or Gas Mark 6

To make the filling:

1. Heat the oil in a medium saucepan, add the onion, leek and garlic, and cook until transparent.

2. Add the wine and tomatoes, cover and continue cooking until tender. Stir in the mascarpone and basil. Season to taste and leave to one side to re-heat when needed.

To make the choux pastry ring:

3. In a heavy-bottomed saucepan, melt the butter with the water. As it begins to boil, remove from the heat.

4. Add the flour and salt and stir with a wooden spoon, mixing thoroughly as it begins to thicken. Add half the cheese, mustard and parsley.

5. Gradually add the eggs to the mixture a little at a time, beating well after each addition. Continue doing this until the mixture no longer looks glossy and all the egg has been absorbed.

6. Using a large dessertspoon, spoon the mixture around the edge of a buttered ovenproof dish.

7. Place in the oven and cook until it is well risen and golden brown, about 15 minutes.

To assemble the gougère:

8. Pour the prepared mixture into the choux ring and sprinkle with the remaining cheese.

9. Place under the grill until the cheese melts and it is golden and bubbling.

Hungarian Goulash with Beans and Brown Ale
can be vegan

A hearty, flavoursome supper dish that can be served with rice, pasta or potatoes.

45ml/3tbsp olive oil
1 large onion, coarsely chopped
2 cloves garlic, crushed
225g/8oz swede, peeled and cubed
1 large red pepper, cut into 1 inch pieces
225g/8oz white cabbage, roughly chopped
30ml/2tbsp unbleached flour
30ml/2tbsp paprika
300ml/½ pint vegan brown ale
300ml/½ pint skimmed milk, or soya milk
15ml/1tbsp cider vinegar
15ml/1tbsp brown sugar
425g/15oz can of cannellini beans or lima, drained
4 gherkins, sliced
salt and freshly ground black pepper
15ml/1tbsp parsley, chopped
150ml/¼ pint sour cream, optional

1. In a large saucepan, heat the oil and gently fry the onions and garlic. Add the swede and continue cooking for 5 minutes. Add the pepper and cabbage and cook for a further 3 minutes.

2. Sprinkle the flour and the paprika over the vegetables and cook for a couple of minutes. Pour the brown ale over the vegetables and wait for any frothing to subside before adding the milk.

3. Stir in the cider vinegar and brown sugar, bring to the boil, then simmer, covered, for about 15 minutes, stirring frequently. Add the beans and continue simmering very gently for a further 5 minutes.

4. Add the sliced gherkins, season to taste and pour the goulash into a serving dish. Top with the chopped parsley and sour cream and serve.

Smoked Tofu Koulibiac

This recipe, a variation on a Russian dish, encases smoked tofu, rice, dill and soured cream in puff pastry.

75g/3oz long grain rice
90ml/3fl oz water
90ml/3fl oz white wine
half a lemon, juice and rind
25g/1oz butter
1 bunch spring onions, chopped
100g/4oz button mushrooms, sliced
225g/8oz smoked tofu, chopped into 1cm/½ inch cubes
5ml/1tsp capers
1 free-range egg, hard-boiled
10ml/2tsp fresh dill, chopped
5ml/1tsp paprika
50g/2oz crème fraiche
450g/1 1b puff pastry
1 egg, beaten

Pre-heat the oven to 200°C, 400°F or Gas Mark 6

1. Cook the rice in the water, wine and lemon juice for 15 minutes or until tender. Drain and reserve.

2. Melt the butter in a medium saucepan and gently sauté the spring onions and mushrooms for 30 minutes or until softened. Add the tofu and cook for a further 5 minutes.

3. Add the cooked rice, capers, chopped egg, fresh dill, lemon rind, paprika and crème fraiche and mix well to combine all the ingredients.

4. On a floured surface, roll out the pastry to a 35cm/14inch square. Place the rice and tofu filling down the centre, leaving 8cm/3 inches of pastry on either side and 5cm/2 inches of pastry at each end. Cut the side borders of pastry diagonally into 2cm/1 inch strips. Brush with beaten egg.

5. Fold both ends of the pastry over the filling, then fold alternate diagonal strips across the filling to create a plait effect. Brush the pastry with the remaining beaten egg, and place the plait on a baking tray. Cook in the pre-heated oven for 30 to 35 minutes, until risen and golden.

Wild Mushroom and Barley Casserole with Cider
vegan

I love barley and its creamy texture. Using wild mushrooms transforms a winter supper into a dinner party dish.

15ml/1tbsp olive oil
1 red onion, chopped
2 cloves garlic, finely chopped
5ml/1tsp dried thyme
4 celery sticks, sliced
225g/8oz mixed mushrooms (button, field, oyster, shitake)
1 red pepper, sliced
175g/6oz pearl barley
450ml/15fl oz vegetable stock
150ml/5fl oz cider
30ml/2tbsp shoyu (soy sauce)
25g/1oz muscovado sugar
5ml/1tsp arrowroot
4 tomatoes, sliced
salt and freshly ground black pepper

1. Heat the oil in a large saucepan and fry the onion gently until softened. Stir in the garlic and thyme and continue cooking for 2 to 3 minutes.

2. Add the celery, mushrooms and red pepper and cook until the mushrooms begin to release their juices. Add the barley, the stock and the cider and stir.

3. In a small bowl, mix together the shoyu and sugar and add this to the casserole.

4. Cover and simmer for about 30 to 40 minutes until the barley is cooked and has absorbed most of the liquid.

5. In a small bowl, mix the arrowroot to a paste with a little water. Add this to the casserole and boil for 1 minute to thicken, stirring all the time.

6. Stir in the parsley and transfer to an ovenproof dish. Arrange the tomato slices on top and place under a hot grill until lightly browned. Serve with a crisp green salad.

Stuffed Onions
can be vegan

In this dish, you can really taste all of the ingredients. The richness of the chestnuts and the freshness of the herbs combine splendidly.

8 medium onions, peeled and left whole
30ml/2tbsp olive oil
2 cloves garlic, finely chopped
I stick celery, chopped finely
50g/2oz tinned chestnuts, chopped coarsely
I0ml/2tsp fresh sage, chopped
5ml/I tsp fresh rosemary, chopped
25g/I oz breadcrumbs
75g/3oz Cheshire cheese (optional)
salt and freshly ground black pepper
To garnish: 30ml/2tbsp chopped fresh parsley

Pre-heat the oven to 190°C, 375°F or Gas Mark 5

1. Bring a large pan of salted water to the boil, add the onions, cover and cook for about 15 minutes. With a sharp knife, hollow out the centre of the onions. Chop half and place on one side (the remainder can be used in a soup or stock).

2. In a medium-sized frying pan, heat 1 tablespoon of olive oil then add the chopped onion centres. Cook for 2 to 3 minutes before adding the garlic and cooking for a further 2 minutes.

3. Add the chopped celery, chestnuts, sage, rosemary, breadcrumbs and seasoning and cook for 5 minutes. Remove from the heat and add the crumbled cheese (if using).

4. Place the onions on a greased baking tray and fill with the stuffing mixture. Drizzle with the other tablespoon of olive oil, place in the oven and cover with foil. Cook for about 20 minutes then remove the foil and cook for a further 10 minutes until the onions are succulent and golden. Serve sprinkled with parsley.

It is easier to chop the cooked onion centres in a food processor as they tend to be very slippery!

Pea and Tomato Rice
vegan

An excellent addition to a vegetarian Chinese meal.

15ml/1 tbsp oil
5ml/1 tsp ground cumin
2 cloves garlic, chopped finely
225g/8oz basmati rice, rinsed and drained in a sieve
15ml/1 tbsp tomato purée
775ml/26fl oz garlic and herb flavoured stock
175g/6oz fresh garden peas or frozen peas, cooked
3 ripe tomatoes, chopped
handful fresh coriander leaves, chopped
freshly ground black pepper

1. Heat the oil in a large frying pan, add the cumin and garlic and fry for 1 minute.

2. Add the rice and stir, then add the tomato purée and cook for a couple of minutes, stirring all the time.

3. Pour in the stock and bring to the boil. Add the seasoning, cover and cook gently for about 10 to 15 minutes until the water is all absorbed.

4. Stir in the peas and tomatoes and heat through, then add the coriander leaves and add more seasoning if required.

Served with chutney, this makes an excellent light lunch.

Mexican Tortilla Casserole with Tangy Green Sauce
can be vegan

This is an unusual savoury recipe using gooseberries to give the authentic tang to the sauce.

350g/12oz fresh or frozen gooseberries
2 green chillies, chopped (leave seeds in)
1 green pepper, de-seeded and chopped
1 small onion, chopped
1 clove garlic, crushed
handful of fresh coriander leaves
30ml/2tbsp lime or lemon juice
15ml/1tbsp apple juice concentrate (or to taste)
60ml/4tbsp sunflower or groundnut oil
12 tortillas, cut or torn into rough triangles
240ml/8fl oz single cream or concentrated soya milk
75g/3oz vegetarian Cheddar cheese (optional)
salt
To garnish: a handful of fresh coriander leaves

1. Place the gooseberries in a saucepan and just cover with water. Bring to the boil and then reduce to a simmer for about 15 minutes. The gooseberries should be soft but still whole. Cool, then place in a food processor or blender and add the chillies, pepper, onion, garlic, coriander and juice. Blend until smooth.

2. Heat the oil and fry the tortilla pieces a few at a time until golden. Drain on kitchen towel.

3. Pour the sauce into the same pan, add the cream or soya milk and cook until it thickens, stirring all the time. Season if necessary.

4. Add about three-quarters of the fried tortilla pieces to the sauce and quickly heat through. Transfer to a heatproof serving dish and top with the cheese if using. Place under a hot grill for a few minutes until golden and bubbling.

5. Sprinkle with chopped coriander and serve with a crisp green salad and the remaining fried tortilla triangles.

The sauce can be chilled and served as an accompaniment to other Mexican dishes.

Braised Tofu
vegan

This is extremely quick and easy to prepare. The tofu is transformed by the flavours of the sauce ingredients.

285g/1 packet firm tofu
30ml/2tbsp vegetable oil
15ml/1tbsp red wine vinegar
30ml/2tbsp shoyu (soy sauce)
10ml/2tsp tomato purée
10ml/2tsp arrowroot
15ml/1tbsp miso
300ml/10fl oz vegetable stock
10ml/2tsp toasted sesame oil

1. Drain the tofu and pat dry with absorbent paper towel. Cut into triangles.

2. Heat the vegetable oil in a frying pan and fry the tofu on both sides until it is golden brown and quite crispy. This will take about 5 minutes. Drain on absorbent paper towel.

3. Return the frying pan to the heat and add the vinegar and shoyu. Add the tomato purée and stir to blend. Blend the arrowroot and miso with the vegetable stock and add to the pan. Bring to the boil and simmer for a couple of minutes, stirring. Finally, add the toasted sesame oil and the tofu pieces and serve immediately with rice or noodles.

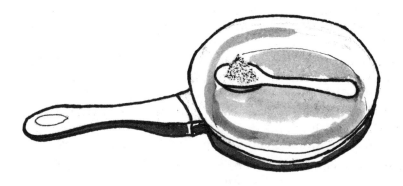

Smoked Tofu Kedgeree

An indispensable recipe - ideal for Sunday brunch, a light lunch or a substantial supper

175g/6oz long grain rice
50g/2oz butter
225g/8oz smoked tofu, *drained and cut into 1cm/½ inch cubes*
pinch cayenne pepper
2 free-range eggs, hard-boiled
60ml/4tbsp parsley, chopped
salt and freshly ground black pepper

1. Cook the rice in slightly salted water until tender. Drain well and spread out on a large plate to cool.

2. Melt the butter in a saucepan and cook the smoked tofu with the cayenne pepper for 5 minutes.

3. Chop one of the hard-boiled eggs and slice the other. Add the chopped egg and cooked rice to the saucepan and heat through.

4. Stir in half the chopped parsley and season to taste. Pile into a warmed serving dish and garnish with the sliced egg and remaining parsley.

Sweet and Sour Broad Beans
vegan

For the best flavour, do try to use fresh broad beans. Serve with
warm crusty bread.

450g/1lb broad beans, shelled (you can use frozen if fresh beans are not available)
30ml/2tbsp vegetable oil
2 cloves garlic, crushed
5ml/1tsp freshly grated ginger
1 bunch spring onions, sliced
1 red pepper, sliced
15ml/1tbsp cornflour
15ml/1tbsp water

For the sauce:

15ml/1tbsp soy sauce
45ml/3tbsp pineapple juice
30ml/2tbsp tomato juice
30ml/2tbsp white wine vinegar
30ml/2tbsp brown sugar

1. Cook the broad beans in boiling salted water until tender.
   Drain and set aside.

2. Place all the sauce ingredients in a pan and heat until the
   sugar has dissolved.

3. Heat the oil in a large frying pan, add the garlic, ginger,
   spring onions and pepper and sauté for 3 to 4 minutes.

4. Add the sauce mixture to the pan and bring to the boil. Make
   a paste with the cornflour and water and add to the sauce.
   Stir until blended, bring to the boil again and cook for a
   further couple of minutes, until the sauce has thickened.
   Add the broad beans and serve.

Butter Bean, Leek and Fennel in a White Wine Sauce

The lemon flavour lifts this dish, enhancing the distinctive taste of the fennel.

2 heads of fennel, trimmed and quartered – reserve the fronds for the garnish
2 bay leaves
the zest of half a lemon
2 leeks, sliced
2 shallots, finely chopped
2 cloves garlic, crushed
200ml/¼ bottle dry white wine
150ml/5fl oz single cream
1 tin butter beans, drained
salt and freshly ground black pepper

1. Place the fennel in a pan, add the bay leaves, lemon zest and seasoning, then add enough water to cover. Bring to the boil and simmer for about 30 minutes, or until the fennel is tender, drain and place in a serving dish.

2. Cook the leeks in boiling water until just tender. Drain and add to the fennel.

3. Place the shallots, garlic and wine in a saucepan and reduce on a low heat until the liquid has almost evaporated. At this stage whisk in the cream and bring to the boil, then simmer gently for 5 minutes. Add the butter beans so they heat through.

4. Pour the sauce over the fennel and leeks and garnish with the fennel fronds. Serve immediately.

Wild Mushroom Pudding
vegan

A tasty variation on traditional suet pudding.
If at all possible, do try to use wild mushrooms – the taste is superior and
the juice they produce is full of flavour.

For the filling:

30ml/2tbsp olive oil
4 shallots, chopped
2 bay leaves
2 cloves garlic, chopped
2 or 3 sprigs fresh thyme
275g/10oz assorted wild mushrooms – if using dried mushrooms, halve the quantity and soak in warm water for 1 hour
120ml/4fl oz red wine
freshly ground black pepper

For the pastry:

225g/8oz self-raising flour
15ml/1tbsp parsley, chopped
100g/4oz vegetable suet
a pinch of salt
120ml/4fl oz water

To prepare the filling:

1. Heat the oil and add the shallots, cook for a few minutes then add the bay leaves and continue cooking over a low heat for 5 minutes.

2. Add the garlic, thyme and mushrooms, cook gently and stir in the wine.

3. Bring to the boil, then simmer gently for 15 minutes and season. Allow to cool.

To make the pastry:

4. Mix the flour, parsley, suet and salt. Add the water gradually and mix with a fork to form a dough.

5. Cut off a quarter of the pastry and reserve for the lid. Knead and roll out the remaining pastry to a circle to line a greased 1.2 litre/2 pint pudding basin.

6. Line the dish with the circle of pastry and fill with the prepared mushroom mixture.

7. Roll out the remaining pastry to form a lid. Dampen the edges of the pastry lining then press the edges of the lining and lid together to seal. Cover with a greased foil top and tie with string.

8. Steam for about 90 minutes, topping up the boiling water to ensure it does not boil dry. Serve with potatoes, mangetout and carrots.

Green Bean Gratin

This recipe works equally well with other fresh vegetables.

450g/1 lb green beans, trimmed
60ml/4tbsp olive oil
225g/8oz mushrooms, sliced
2 cloves garlic, chopped
a handful of flat-leaf parsley, chopped
2 tomatoes, chopped
30ml/2tbsp fresh breadcrumbs
75g/3oz Gruyère cheese, grated
5ml/1tsp fresh rosemary, chopped
salt and freshly ground black pepper

Pre-heat the oven to 200°C, 400°F or Gas Mark 6

1. Blanch the beans in boiling water, drain and set aside.

2. Heat 2tbsp of oil in a medium-sized pan and fry the mushrooms and garlic. Add the seasoning and parsley.

3. Add the green beans and tomatoes and heat gently in the oil for a couple of minutes.

4. Pour the mixture into an ovenproof dish. Mix together the breadcrumbs, cheese and rosemary and sprinkle over the mushrooms and green beans.

5. Drizzle the remaining olive oil over the dish and place in the oven for about 25 minutes, until golden.

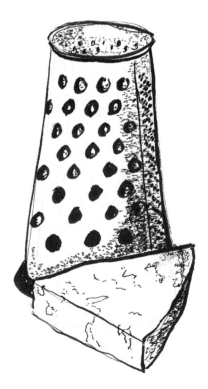

Roast Vegetable Torte

This dish is extremely simple to prepare, though rather indulgent. Enjoy it served with a continental salad and a glass of Rioja.

3 peppers – yellow, red and green – cubed
2 medium courgettes, cubed
1 medium aubergine, cubed
1 tin artichoke hearts, drained and halved
1 onion, chopped
4 bay leaves
2 sprigs rosemary
2 sprigs oregano
75ml/5tbsp olive oil
225g/8oz ricotta cheese
4 free-range eggs, beaten
5ml/1tsp salt
15ml/1tbsp dried mixed Italian herbs

Pre-heat the oven to 200°C, 400°F or Gas Mark 6

1. Place the vegetables and fresh herbs on a grilling tray and pour the olive oil over. Turn the vegetables to coat them and then grill for 10 to 15 minutes, until the vegetables start to brown.

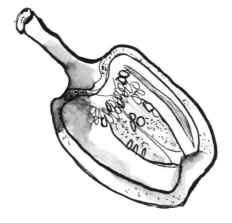

2. Combine the grilled vegetables with the cheese, eggs, salt and mixed Italian herbs.

3. Pack the mixture into a 25cm/10 inch flan dish and bake for 30 minutes.

Polenta with Sun-Dried Tomatoes

An excellent way to serve polenta as it requires plenty of added flavour.

40ml/2.5tbsp olive oil
3 cloves garlic, finely chopped
5ml/1tsp dried sage
100g/4oz polenta
100g/4oz sun-dried tomatoes, chopped finely
¼ red chilli, chopped finely
240ml/8fl oz oat milk
450ml/15fl oz water
oil, to brush on before grilling
100g/4oz vegetarian Cheddar cheese
salt, to taste

1. Heat the oil in a large, heavy pan and add the garlic, sage and salt. Stir until the garlic starts to colour a little, then add the polenta and stir for a few more minutes.

2. Add the sun-dried tomatoes and chilli and stir for a few minutes. Remove from the heat and leave the pan to cool a little.

3. While the pan is off the heat, add all the oat milk and half of the water, stirring it in gradually. The polenta will begin to thicken a little. Stir continually, keeping the mixture lump free.

4. Return the pan to the heat and, stirring all the time, add the remaining water. The polenta is cooked when it is no longer granular and is as thick as you can make it without it sticking or burning.

5. Transfer the polenta to a square casserole dish (about 18cm/7 inches square) and leave for about 1 hour to set.

6. Slice the polenta into the desired shapes, brush with a little oil and sprinkle with cheese. Grill and serve hot with rocket and a tomato salsa.

Baked New Potato Salad
vegan

This recipe is easy to prepare and tasty – ideal for summer meals.
Serve it in small bowls on a bed of mixed leaves.

24 Jersey Royal potatoes
virgin olive oil
a bunch of chives
I lemon, zest and juice
10 sage leaves, chopped
salt and freshly ground black pepper
mixed leaves, *e.g. lamb's lettuce, rocket or curly endive*

Pre-heat the oven to 180°C, 350°F or Gas Mark 4

1. Lightly steam the potatoes for 5 minutes then transfer them
   to a roasting tin lined with foil.

2. Drizzle some oil over the potatoes and then add the chives,
   lemon zest, sage and salt and pepper. Fold the foil to make a
   sealed parcel.

3. Cook in the oven for 45 minutes. Meanwhile make a dressing
   by mixing the lemon juice with 3-4 tablespoons of oil. Serve
   the potatoes on the mixed leaves while they are still hot,
   drizzling the dressing over at the last minute.

Spinach and Smoked Tofu Salad
vegan

A quick nutritious dish. The smoked tofu, cooked with the tamari,
gives it a wonderfully distinctive taste.

225g/8oz smoked tofu, drained
30ml/2tbsp tamari
15ml/1tbsp groundnut oil
175g/6oz fresh baby spinach leaves
6 spring onions, cut finely on the slant
2 peaches, stoned and sliced
50g/2oz walnut halves
1 clove garlic, crushed
10ml/2tsp olive oil
2 slices granary bread
45ml/3tbsp sesame oil
15ml/1tbsp cider vinegar
10ml/2tsp apple juice concentrate
salt and freshly ground black pepper

1. Cut the smoked tofu into thin slices, arrange on a plate and
   sprinkle with the tamari sauce. Leave to marinate for 10
   minutes.

2. Drain off the tamari and fry the strips in the groundnut oil
   for 3 to 4 minutes on each side, until they are brown and
   slightly crispy. Remove, and drain on kitchen paper.

3. Place the spinach, spring onions, peaches and walnuts in a
   bowl. Mix the crushed garlic in the olive oil. Brush both
   sides of the bread with the garlic oil and toast on both sides
   until golden. Cut into crouton-sized pieces and add to the
   salad bowl.

4. Combine the sesame oil, vinegar and apple juice. Season to
   taste.

5. Cut the smoked tofu strips into bite-sized pieces and add to
   the salad bowl.

6. Dress the salad and serve in individual dishes.

Spicy Noodles with Spring Vegetables and Spicy Peanut Sauce
vegan

A colourful dish which looks impressive yet takes very little time to prepare.

I packet noodles
3 courgettes, cut into matchsticks
3 carrots, cut into matchsticks
175g/6oz green beans
30ml/2tbsp peanut oil (groundnut oil)
I bunch spring onions
2 cloves garlic, crushed
I bunch radishes (halved if large)
450g/1lb mushrooms
I red pepper, de-seeded and cut into strips
coriander to garnish

For the sauce:

30ml/2tbsp groundnut oil
I large chilli, chopped
15ml/1tbsp lemon juice
30ml/2tbsp sugar
45ml/3tbsp ground roasted peanuts
180ml/6fl oz coconut milk

1. Cook the noodles as directed on the packet, refresh and set aside. Keep warm.
2. Steam the courgettes, carrots and green beans and put to one side.
3. Heat the oil in a wok and stir-fry the spring onions, garlic, radishes, mushrooms and red pepper for 5 minutes. Remove the vegetables with a slotted spoon and set aside. Keep warm.

To make the sauce:

4. Heat the oil in the wok, add the chilli and fry for 2 to 3 minutes so it blends with the oil.
5. Add the rest of the ingredients and stir constantly until a thick sauce is formed.
6. To serve, arrange the noodles on a large serving plate, pile the vegetables on top then cover with the sauce. Garnish with the coriander.

Spinach and Pear Plait

Spinach and pear make a wonderful combination, and in this recipe the flavours are greatly enhanced by the addition of the blue cheese.

4 shallots, sliced thickly
I clove garlic, unpeeled
75g/3oz pecan nuts, chopped
2 pears, cored and sliced
450g/1lb fresh spinach
225g/8oz puff pastry
100g/4oz Roquefort cheese
a pinch of freshly ground nutmeg
I free-range egg, beaten
salt and freshly ground black pepper

Pre-heat the oven to 200°C, 400°F or Gas Mark 6

1. Place the shallots, garlic, nuts and pears on a greased baking tray. Roast in the oven for 10 minutes. Remove the garlic from its skin and mix all the ingredients together, seasoning to taste.

2. Wash the spinach and cook it in the water that is remaining on the leaves only. Do not allow the spinach to become soggy. Drain and set aside.

3. Roll out the puff pastry to about 20cm/8 inches x 30cm/12 inches. Place the spinach down the centre, sprinkle with nutmeg, then top with the roasted ingredients. Place the pieces of Roquefort on top of the mixture.

4. Cut the pastry on either side of the filling into 2.5cm/1 inch diagonal strips, leaving at least half an inch uncut on either side of the filling. Using the strips from alternate sides, plait the pastry.

5. Brush with egg and place in the oven for about 20 minutes, until golden.

Sausage, Apple and Stilton Pie

My favourite pie! This recipe has been modified over the years – usually to suit whatever was in the refrigerator at the time! So don't be afraid to experiment with the ingredients.

350g/12oz plain flour
15ml/1tbsp dried sage
175g/6oz butter, cubed
15ml/1tbsp olive oil
1 onion, peeled and chopped
2 cloves garlic, crushed
50g/2oz mushrooms, sliced
275g/10oz spinach, cooked
2 tomatoes, sliced
2 cooking apples, cored and sliced
4 vegetarian sausages, lightly grilled and sliced
275g/10oz vegetarian Stilton, crumbled
1 free-range egg yolk, beaten, to glaze
salt and freshly ground black pepper

Pre-heat the oven to 200°C, 400°F or Gas Mark 6

1. Sift the flour and a pinch of salt in a large bowl and stir in the sage. Then rub the butter into the flour until it resembles breadcrumbs.

2. Stir in six tablespoons of cold water with a knife until the pastry is combined. Turn out onto a floured board and knead gently. Wrap in cling film and place in the refrigerator for 30 minutes.

3. Meanwhile, heat the oil in a medium-sized pan and fry the onion and garlic for 5 minutes. Add the mushrooms and cook for 5 minutes. Season.

4. Roll out two-thirds of the pastry and use to line the base of a non-stick, loose-bottomed 24cm/9 inch flan tin.

5. Spread the mushroom mixture over the bottom, followed by the spinach then the tomatoes. Continue with a layer of apple followed by the sausage and finally top with the cheese.

6. Roll out the remaining pastry and use to top the pie, sealing the edges with a little water. Glaze with the egg yolk.

7. Bake for about 40 minutes or until golden brown. Serve with new potatoes and a herb salad.

Asparagus and Baby Sweetcorn Pithiviers with a Watercress Sauce
vegan

The name Pithivier refers to the town in France where this kind of tart originated. Traditionally it is all cooked together, but here I have pre-cooked the puff pastry cases.

For the watercress sauce:

25g/1oz vegan margarine
3 spring onions, chopped
300ml/10fl oz vegetable stock
2 bunches watercress, chopped
salt and freshly ground black pepper

For the pithiviers:

375g/13oz packet of ready-rolled puff pastry
30ml/2tbsp soya milk
50g/2oz sesame seeds

For the filling:

2 garlic cloves, left whole and with skins
1 bunch asparagus, chopped into 5cm/2 inch pieces
1 packet baby sweetcorn, chopped into 5cm/2 inch pieces
50g/2oz vegan margarine
50g/2oz unbleached flour
390ml/13fl oz soya milk
90ml/3fl oz vegan white wine
75g/3oz ground pine nuts, roasted
5ml/1tsp mustard
1 handful fresh, flat-leaf parsley, chopped (reserve a few leaves to garnish)

Pre-heat the oven to 180°C, 350°F or Gas Mark 4

To make the watercress sauce:

1. Heat the margarine and fry the spring onions until soft.

2. Add the stock and bring to the boil, simmer for 5 minutes.

3. Add the watercress, boil for 15 seconds, then remove from the heat. Season to taste.

4. Cool, then blend until smooth. Turn into a clean pan and reheat when ready to serve.

To prepare the pithiviers:

5. To prepare the cases, place the ready-rolled pastry on a lightly floured board and cut out 4 rounds with a 13cm/5 inch plain cutter.

6. Place the pastry rounds on a greased baking sheet, brush with soya milk and sprinkle with sesame seeds.

7. Place in the oven for 15 minutes until well risen and golden brown. Remove from the oven and place on one side to keep warm.

To make the filling:

8. Place the garlic cloves in the oven for about 10 minutes. When you take them out of the oven it should be easy to remove them from their skins. Place the garlic on one side.

9. Meanwhile, steam the asparagus and sweetcorn until just tender, then leave to one side.

10. Melt the vegan margarine in a large saucepan, add the flour and stir. Cook the roux for 1 to 2 minutes, stirring continually. Remove from the heat and add the soya milk, stirring all the time. Place back on the heat and continue to stir until the sauce thickens, at this point add the wine and continue stirring. Cook for a couple of minutes then remove from the heat. (The sauce should be quite thick.)

11. Mix together the pine nuts, mustard and roasted garlic and add to the sauce, beating constantly.

12. Add the parsley and the vegetables to the sauce.

13. To assemble, cut the pastry cases horizontally in half and remove the pastry inside. Place some of the vegetable mixture on each of the pastry bases and top with the pastry lids.

14. To serve, place a pithivier in the centre of each plate and pour some of the heated watercress sauce around it. Garnish with the parsley and serve immediately.

Mushroom Stroganoff

You probably have a favourite Stroganoff recipe, but I thoroughly
recommend this one – it is excellent.

Serves 4 to 6

For the rice:

175g/6oz long grain brown rice (washed)
50g/2oz wild rice
15ml/1 tbsp sunflower oil
600ml/1 pint water
5ml/1 tsp turmeric
2 bay leaves

For the Stroganoff:

15ml/1 tbsp sunflower oil
1 large onion, peeled and finely chopped
4 sticks celery, chopped
2 leeks, cleaned and sliced
350g/12oz mushrooms, cleaned and chopped
50g/2oz butter or margarine
15ml/1 tbsp wholewheat flour
150ml/5fl oz light vegetable stock
2.5ml/½tsp dried thyme (or 5ml/1 tsp fresh thyme)
150ml/5fl oz soured cream
salt and freshly ground black pepper
chopped parsley, to garnish

To prepare the rice:

1. Toast the rice in the oil for 2 minutes. Add the water,
turmeric and bay leaves, bring to the boil, stir and cover.
Simmer for 20 to 25 minutes, until just cooked. Drain if
necessary.

To prepare the Stroganoff:

2. Cook the Stroganoff just before it is required.

3. Heat the oil in a large saucepan and fry the onion until soft but not brown, add the celery and leeks and cook for a further 3 minutes. Add the mushrooms and cook for another 2 or 3 minutes.

4. Add the margarine, allow to melt then stir in the flour. Cook for 1 minute. Remove from the heat and add the stock and herbs. Bring to the boil, stirring all the time. Simmer for 3 or 4 minutes.

5. Season, and just before serving, add the sour cream (do not boil again after the cream has been added).

6. Arrange the rice in a ring on a large plate and pour the Stroganoff into the centre. Sprinkle with chopped parsley and serve at once.

Fattoush
can be vegan

This is a variation on the traditional Lebanese bread salad.

For the croutons:

1 clove garlic, peeled but left whole
2 thin slices bread, toasted
30ml/2tbsp olive oil
10ml/2tsp fresh mint, finely chopped

For the dressing:

the juice of half a lemon
30ml/2tbsp olive oil
5ml/1tsp wholegrain mustard
1 clove garlic, crushed

For the salad:

1 iceberg lettuce, shredded
75g/3oz walnuts, halved
4 tomatoes, quartered
1/4 cucumber, cubed
4 spring onions, finely chopped
10 capers
2 fresh peaches, quartered
225g/8oz new potatoes, cooked
25g/1oz black olives, pitted and halved
15ml/1tbsp fresh mint, finely chopped
15ml/1tbsp fresh parsley, finely chopped
425g/15oz tin chick peas OR
75g/3oz vegetarian feta cheese, diced (omit for vegans)

Pre-heat the oven to 180°C, 350°F or Gas Mark 4

1. Rub the peeled garlic over the surface of the toasted bread. Mix the olive oil and chopped mint and brush over the surface of the bread. Place on a baking tray and bake for 5 minutes. Remove the crusts and cut into small croutons.

2. Mix all the dressing ingredients together.

3. Mix all the salad ingredients together in a large bowl and toss with the dressing.

4. Transfer to a serving dish and sprinkle with the croutons. Serve at once.
    If using the feta cheese, soak it in the dressing before adding to the salad.

Haggis
vegan

Vegetarians don't have to miss the highlight of a Burns' Night supper with this simple alternative.

100g/4oz onion, peeled and finely chopped
15ml/1tbsp sunflower oil
50g/2oz carrots, very finely chopped
35g/1½oz mushrooms, finely chopped
50g/2oz red lentils
600ml/1 pint light vegetable stock
25g/1oz mashed, tinned red kidney beans
35g/1½oz ground peanuts
25g/1oz ground hazelnuts
30ml/2tbsp shoyu
15ml/1tbsp lemon juice
7.5ml/1½tsp dried thyme
5ml/1tsp dried rosemary
7.5ml/1½tsp cayenne pepper
7.5ml/1½tsp mixed spice
200g/8oz fine oatmeal
freshly ground black pepper

Pre-heat the oven to 190°C, 375°F or Gas Mark 5

1. Sauté the onion in the oil for 5 minutes, then add the carrot and mushrooms and cook for a further 5 minutes.

2. Now add the lentils and three-quarters of the stock.

3. Blend the mashed red kidney beans in the remaining stock, and add these to the pan with the nuts, shoyu, lemon juice and seasonings. Cook everything, well mixed together, for a further 10 to 15 minutes.

4. Then add the oatmeal, reduce the heat and simmer gently for 15 to 20 minutes, adding a little extra liquid if necessary.

5. Turn the mixture into a lightly oiled 450g/1lb loaf tin and bake for 30 minutes.

Stuffed Vine Leaves
vegan

I've added apricots and currants to the stuffing as they marry so well with the mint.

175g/6oz bulgar wheat
5ml/1tsp salt
360ml/12fl oz boiling water
60ml/2fl oz olive oil
60ml/2fl oz lemon juice
60ml/4tbsp fresh mint, finely chopped
60ml/4tbsp fresh parsley, finely chopped
2 or 3 cloves garlic, crushed
1 bunch spring onions, thinly sliced
3 sun-dried tomatoes, chopped finely
1/2 cucumber, chopped finely
50g/2oz dried apricots, chopped finely
50g/2oz currants
175g/6oz vine leaves
60ml/2fl oz white wine
freshly ground black pepper

Pre-heat the oven to 180°C, 350°F or Gas Mark 4

1. Mix the bulgar wheat and salt in a bowl. Pour over the boiling water and stir. Leave to stand for 15 minutes.

2. Make a dressing with the olive oil, lemon juice, mint, parsley and garlic. Pour over the soaked bulgar and leave for a couple of hours for the flavours to combine.

3. Stir in the spring onion, sun-dried tomato, cucumber, apricots and currants.

4. Blanch the vine leaves in boiling water for 5 minutes to soften them. Rinse in cold water and drain.

5. To fill the vine leaves, place a leaf vein-side up and put a small amount of filling on it. Roll up like a small cigar, tucking in the sides as you roll. Start rolling from the stalk end.

6. Lightly oil an ovenproof dish and pack the vine leaves tightly in. Sprinkle with black pepper, pour over the white wine and cover with foil. Cook for about 45 minutes. Serve hot or cold.

Caerphilly, Celery and Macadamia Tart

A subtle but interesting combination of flavours and textures. For a stronger, more distinctive taste, try a blue cheese instead of the Caerphilly.

220g/8oz ready-made shortcrust pastry
1 free-range egg
120ml/4 fl oz single cream
75g/3oz Caerphilly, crumbled
30ml/2tbsp chopped fresh chives
25g/1oz macadamia nuts, chopped
2 sticks celery, chopped
5ml/1tsp fresh marjoram, chopped

Pre-heat the oven to 220°C, 425°F or Gas Mark 7

1. Cut the pastry into 4 pieces. Roll out each piece and use to line four 10cm/4 inch fluted tart tins. Prick the pastry with a fork and bake in the oven for 10 minutes.

2. Meanwhile, beat the egg with the cream and stir in the cheese, chives, nuts, celery and marjoram.

3. Spoon the mixture into the pastry cases, return to the oven and bake for a further 10 minutes or until set and golden in colour. Serve hot or cold.

Smoked Cheese Potato Cake with Red Onion Confit

A classic dish from the Loire valley.

50g/2oz butter
2 cloves garlic, crushed
60ml/4tbsp parsley, finely chopped
900g/2lb potatoes, peeled and sliced
175g/6oz smoked cheese, thinly sliced
freshly grated nutmeg
a handful of flat-leaf parsley, to garnish

For the confit:

30ml/2tbsp olive oil
2 red onions
50g/2oz brown sugar
150ml/5fl oz red wine
salt and freshly ground black pepper

Pre-heat the oven to 190°C, 375°F or Gas Mark 5

1. Grease a 20cm/8 inch soufflé dish with the butter and sprinkle with the crushed garlic and some of the parsley.

2. Place layers of half the potatoes, cheese and parsley in the dish. Season well and sprinkle with the nutmeg. Repeat the layers, ending with a layer of cheese.

3. Place foil over the dish and bake in the oven for about 50 minutes or until the potato is cooked.

4. Turn out on to a serving plate and serve with the red onion confit. Garnish with the parsley.

5. To make the red onion confit, heat the oil in a medium-sized pan and sweat the onions on a low heat for 10 minutes or until just browning.

6. Add the sugar and stir until caramelised. Add the wine and stew on a low heat for about 40 minutes.

Asparagus and Roasted Red Pepper Salad
vegan

The flavour of peppers intensifies tremendously when roasted. I always roast peppers in advance as they can be stored in the refrigerator for a couple of days.

I large red pepper
I large yellow pepper
450g/1lb asparagus, lightly steamed
I medium red apple, cored and sliced
I medium green apple, cored and sliced
30ml/2tbsp lemon juice
30ml/2tbsp lime juice
a handful of flat-leaf parsley, chopped
a pinch of chilli powder
salt and freshly ground black pepper

Pre-heat the oven to 220°C, 425°F or Gas Mark 7

1. Place the peppers on an oiled baking sheet and roast until the skins are black. Place in a plastic bag and leave until cool.

2. Meanwhile, cut the cooked asparagus into 5cm/2 inch pieces and place in a bowl. Add the apple and mix together.

3. Mix the lemon and lime juices together and season. Pour over the asparagus and apple and mix well to stop the apple browning.

4. Remove the skins from the peppers and discard the stem and seeds. Cut into strips and add to the asparagus and apple.

5. Add the parsley. Toss the salad gently then sprinkle with the chilli powder.

Pasta Sauces

I have chosen a small selection of sauce recipes which are new and
different, and which should allow you to ring the changes during the seasons.

Pumpkin Sauce
can be vegan

15ml/1 tbsp olive oil
25g/1oz butter or vegan margarine
2 cloves garlic, chopped
675g/1 ½ lb pumpkin flesh, cubed
600ml/1pt vegetable stock
black pepper

1. Heat the oil and the butter in a large pan and fry the garlic
   for a couple of minutes.

2. Add the pumpkin and stir in a small amount of the stock.
   Cover and cook over a low heat for about 15 minutes, until
   the pumpkin is cooked.

3. Leave to cool and then place in a liquidizer and blend,
   adding the stock as you go along, until the desired
   consistency for the sauce has been achieved.

4. Re-heat, season with lots of black pepper and serve with
   your favourite pasta.

Fresh Sage Sauce

50g/2oz butter
50g/2oz shallots, peeled and finely chopped
150ml/5fl oz dry vermouth
50g/2oz flour
150ml/5fl oz single cream
150ml/5fl oz garlic stock – use a cube
30ml/2tbsp freshly chopped sage leaves

1. Melt the butter in a medium-sized saucepan, and cook the shallots until softened.

2. Add the vermouth and reduce the sauce until slightly thickened.

3. Stir in the flour and cook for 1 minute, stirring continually. Add the cream and stock and simmer until thickened. Stir in the sage leaves and cook for a further 2 minutes. Serve with your favourite pasta shapes.

Almond Sauce
vegan

30ml/2tbsp olive oil
a pinch of cayenne pepper
1 large onion, peeled and chopped
50g/2oz mushrooms, chopped
half a green pepper, finely chopped
2 or 3 cloves garlic, crushed
75g/3oz ground almonds
150ml/5fl oz water
1 vegetable stock cube
salt and freshly ground black pepper

1. Heat the oil in a medium-sized pan and sauté the cayenne pepper, onion, mushrooms, green pepper and garlic over a low heat for 5 minutes.

2. Blend the ground almonds and water in a blender, add the stock cube and blend for a further 30 seconds, until completely smooth.

3. Pour the sauce over the vegetable mixture and slowly heat through, stirring all the time to prevent burning. The mixture will thicken considerably.

4. Take half the mixture and blend until smooth, being careful not to overprocess or the sauce will resemble a soup. Return to the pan and combine with the rest of the sauce.

5. Season to taste, and pour over your favourite pasta.

Red Hot Sauce
vegan

15ml/1 tbsp vegetable oil
1 onion, peeled and finely chopped
3 cloves garlic, crushed
3 chillies, de-seeded and chopped finely
1 red pepper, finely chopped
50g/2oz mushrooms, sliced
3 tomatoes, peeled and chopped
30ml/2tbsp passata (sieved tomatoes)
15ml/1 tbsp fresh coriander, chopped

1. Heat the oil in a large saucepan and add the onion. Cook until softened then add the garlic.

2. Add the chillies and pepper and cook gently for 2 or 3 minutes. Add the mushrooms and cook for a further 5 minutes.

3. Add the tomatoes and passata and simmer for 10 to 15 minutes. Stir in the coriander.

4. Toss with your favourite pasta shape.

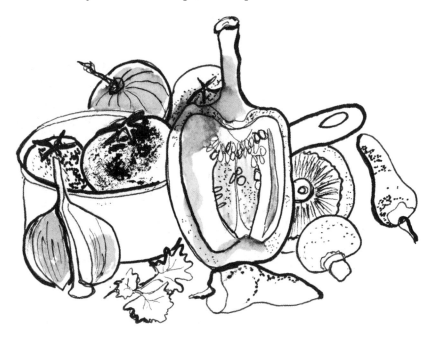

Desserts

Poached Pears with Red Wine and Ginger Sauce
vegan

Poached pear recipes are always popular. This one is distinguished by the addition of ginger.

4 hard pears
300ml/10fl oz red wine
25g/1oz caster sugar
1 whole cinnamon stick
5ml/1tsp arrowroot
1 piece stem ginger, very finely chopped
15ml/1tbsp stem ginger syrup

1. Peel the pears, but leave the stalks intact.

2. Slice a thin disc from the base of each pear, if necessary, to make it sit upright.

3. Place the pears on their sides in a saucepan. Pour in the red wine, sprinkle over the sugar and add the cinnamon stick.

4. Bring up to simmering point, cover the pan and simmer very slowly for about one hour, turning now and again so that the pears cook evenly in the wine.

5. When the pears are cooked, transfer to a bowl to cool, leaving the poaching liquid in the pan. Remove the cinnamon stick.

6. Mix the arrowroot with a little water until it forms a smooth paste. Add this to the liquid in the pan over direct heat. Bring the syrup just up to simmering point so that it thickens slightly and becomes translucent.

7. Take the pan off the heat and stir in the chopped stem ginger and ginger syrup to taste. Leave to cool. Spoon the sauce over the pears, basting them well. Cover and chill thoroughly. Serve the pears in individual dishes with the sauce spooned over.

Baked Tofu Cake
vegan

This is easier than a baked cheesecake to prepare but full of flavour.

For the base:

225g/8oz digestive biscuit crumbs
100g/4oz vegan margarine

For the topping:

450g/1lb silken tofu
1 orange – zest only
150g/5oz dates, cooked with a little water and liquidized
120ml/4fl oz apple juice concentrate
5ml/1tsp cinnamon
15ml/1tbsp Cointreau
extra fruit for decoration

Pre-heat the oven to 180°C, 350°F or Gas Mark 4

To make the base:

1. Melt the margarine and stir in the biscuit crumbs.
2. Grease a 25cm/9inch flan tin and spread the mixture over the base, pushing lightly into the edges.

To make the topping:

3. Blend all the ingredients together in a liquidizer and pour over the base.
4. Bake for about 40 minutes. Allow to cool, then chill.
5. Decorate with extra fresh fruit.

Crème de l'Afrique

This dessert is very special - an irresistible combination of flavours.

Serves 3 or 4

For the apricot purée:

12 dried sour apricots
juice of 2 medium mandarins

For the crème:

50g/2oz smooth peanut butter
150g/5oz fromage frais
30ml/2tbsp runny honey
10ml/2tsp unsalted butter, melted
180ml/6fl oz whipping cream

For the chocolate topping:

90ml/3fl oz whipping cream
100g/4oz milk chocolate, chopped
thick cream for topping
coffee liqueur

To make the apricot purée:

1. Soak the apricots in the mandarin juice for 30 minutes.
   Blend until smooth then spoon into dessert glasses.

To make the crème:

2. Blend the peanut butter, fromage frais and honey until
   smooth, then add the melted butter.

3. Whip the cream until it forms peaks and fold into the peanut
   butter mixture.

4. Spoon the crème on top of the apricot purée and refrigerate.

To make the chocolate topping:

5. Put the cream and chopped chocolate in a saucepan and melt gently on a low heat.

6. Allow the chocolate topping to cool a little, then spoon it over the crème and return the glasses to the fridge.

7. Before serving pour a little coffee liqueur over each dessert and top with a blob of thick cream. Add your own preferred decoration – chocolate flakes, a sprig of mint or orange zest, for example.

Chocolate Pots
vegan

An easy dessert to make when time is short. The combnation of dark chocolate and orange never fails.

100g/4oz dark vegan chocolate *plus a little extra for decoration*
250g/9oz packet silken tofu
15ml/1tbsp Cointreau or rum or brandy
the grated zest and juice of ½ an orange
15-30ml/1-2tbsp maple syrup, to taste

1. Melt the chocolate in a bowl over a pan of just simmering water.

2. Put the tofu, chosen liqueur and orange juice into a liquidizer and blend until smooth.

3. Add the melted chocolate and maple syrup then blend again.

4. Pour into four ramekins and chill for at least one hour. Decorate with grated chocolate and orange zest.

'Maja Bianca' Pudding
can be vegan

This is a traditional Filipino dessert which was introduced by Spanish colonists 450 years ago. Traditionally it is served on fresh banana leaves. Tropical fruits and nuts can be added to enhance the flavour.

75g/3oz cornflour
75g/3oz sugar (or to taste)
90ml/3fl oz milk or soya milk
7.5ml/½tbsp vanilla essence
180ml/6fl oz coconut milk
325g/11oz can creamed sweetcorn

1. In a small mixing bowl, blend the cornflour, sugar, milk and vanilla essence.

2. Put the coconut milk and creamed sweetcorn into a medium saucepan and mix well over heat.

3. Slowly add the cornflour mixture, stirring constantly until the mixture thickens. Remove from the heat.

4. Cool, stir and pour into a mould, ramekin dishes or a rectangular cake tin. Leave to stand and set. Chill before serving.

Ruby Grapefruit, Melon and Ginger Fruit Salad
vegan

A light and refreshing conclusion to a rich dinner party menu, and the ideal dessert for a warm summer evening.

2 Galia or Ogen melons
2 ruby grapefruits
1 star fruit
2 pieces ginger – bottled in syrup
30ml/2tbsp syrup from the ginger
mint leaves to garnish
soya or dairy cream to serve (optional)

1. Use a melon baller or chop the flesh of the melon into attractive shapes.

2. Peel and segment the grapefruits, removing all the pith and pips and reserving about 40ml/2½ tablespoons of the juice.

3. Slice the star fruit thinly and mix all the fruits and juice together.

4. Finely chop the ginger and toss the fruit in the ginger and syrup. Leave to marinate for 1 to 2 hours.

5. Place in glass serving dishes and decorate with mint leaves. Can be served with soya or dairy cream.

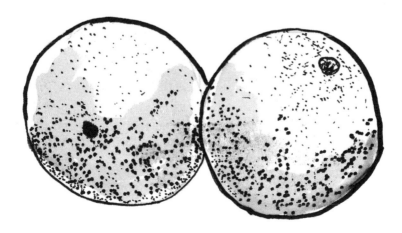

Apple and Orange Tatin
vegan

The flavour and texture of this tatin are enhanced by the addition of cinnamon, orange and nuts.

Serves 6

For the base:

100g/4oz hard vegan margarine, cut into small cubes
200g/7oz plain, unbleached white flour
25g/1oz icing sugar
5ml/1tsp ground cinnamon
1 orange, finely grated rind and juice

For the topping:

50g/2oz vegan margarine
900g/2lb cooking apples, peeled, cored and cut into 2.5cm/1inch chunks
50-75g/2-3oz soft brown sugar
1 orange, rind in thin strips and juice
50g/2oz chopped mixed nuts

Pre-heat the oven to 200°C, 400°F or Gas Mark 6

To make the base:

1. Rub the margarine into the flour until the mixture resembles breadcrumbs.

2. Mix in the sugar, cinnamon and orange rind. Add enough orange juice to form a medium dough. Cover and chill in the fridge.

To make the topping:

3. Melt the margarine in a heavy-based frying pan and gently sauté the apples and brown sugar for 2 minutes. Add the orange rind, juice and chopped nuts.

4. Continue cooking the apples for a few minutes more until the sauce becomes syrupy and the apples have softened a little.

5. Place the apples and syrup in the base of a greased 22.5cm/9 inch spring form tin.

6. Remove the dough from the fridge and roll out roughly on a floured board. The dough needs to be only slightly larger than the tin. Place the dough over the apples, tucking any excess down the sides of the tin.

7. Bake for 25 to 30 minutes until the crust is golden brown. Invert the tatin on a serving plate and enjoy!

Baked Bananas with Plum Sauce
vegan

Very simple and a firm favourite with all ages.

4 large bananas
pinch ground cloves or cinnamon
300ml/10fl oz orange juice
450g/1lb red plums
10ml/2tsp dark raw cane sugar

Pre-heat the oven to 180°C, 350°F or Gas Mark 4

1. Peel the bananas, slice lengthways and arrange in an ovenproof dish. Sprinkle the ground cloves or cinnamon over the bananas and pour on the orange juice. Bake in the oven for about 20 minutes.

2. Meanwhile, wash, halve and stone the plums. Cook in a saucepan with a little water and the sugar.

3. When the plums are tender, liquidize, mash with a potato masher, or push through a sieve to produce a smooth sauce. Heat gently and pour into a jug to serve.

In winter, a can of plums can be used.

Blackcurrant and Apple Pie in a Coconut Pastry
vegan

The subtle flavour of coconut in the pastry makes this traditional pie something memorable. Of course you could substitute any seasonal fruits of your choice.

Serves 6 to 8

For the pastry:

25g/1oz caster sugar
50g/2oz creamed coconut (grated)
100g/4oz plain flour
100g/4oz self-raising flour
100g/4oz vegan margarine

For the filling:

75g/3oz caster sugar
40g/1½oz cornflour
450g/1lb blackcurrants (fresh, frozen or tinned), thawed and drained
30ml/2tbsp desiccated coconut or ground almonds
2 eating apples, sliced very finely (sprinkle with lemon juice to prevent browning)

Pre-heat the oven to 200°C, 400°F or Gas Mark 6

To make the pastry:

1. Mix the sugar and coconut cream in a small dish. Add approximately 45-60ml/3 to 4 tablespoons boiling water and stir the mixture to form a cream.

2. Sieve the flour into a bowl, cut the margarine into small pieces and, using your fingertips, rub the margarine into the flour until it resembles breadcrumbs. Make a well in the centre, add the dissolved coconut cream and combine it with the flour to form a soft dough. Chill for 20 minutes.

To make the filling:

3. In a bowl mix together the caster sugar and cornflour, add the blackcurrants and mix gently to coat the blackcurrants (check sweetness).

4. Take two thirds of the pastry and roll out to line a 22.5ml/9 inch pie dish. Scatter the desiccated coconut or almonds on the base of pastry, place the sliced apple on the coconut and then add the blackcurrants. Pour any remaining liquid over the currants.

5. Roll out the remaining pastry for the top of the dish. Wet the edges of the base pastry with water, place the rolled out pastry on top and seal the edges by pressing together with a fork. Cut a small hole in the centre to let out steam and use any spare pastry to decorate the top of the pie.

6. Brush the top of the pie with milk or egg wash and dust with caster sugar.

7. Place in the pre-heated oven for 20 minutes, then reduce the heat to 160°C, 325°F or Gas Mark 3 for 20 minutes – until the pie is golden brown and bubbling. Dust again with caster sugar and allow to cool before cutting.

Californian Orange Tart
vegan

It is vital to begin the preparation of this dish the day before it is required as the orange slices must stand overnight in the sugar syrup.

Serves 6 to 8

For the pastry:

175g/6oz plain flour
75g/3oz vegan margarine
35g/1 ¼oz icing sugar

For the filling:

75g/3oz vegan chocolate
750ml/25fl oz soya milk
12ml/¾tbsp custard powder
300ml/10fl oz pure orange juice
10ml/2tsp agar flakes
50g/2oz caster sugar
15ml/1tbsp vegan margarine

For the topping:

2 small oranges
300ml/10fl oz water
150g/5oz caster sugar
60ml/4tbsp apricot jam

Pre-heat the oven to 200°C, 400°F or Gas Mark 6

To prepare the topping:

1. Thinly slice the oranges (.25cm/⅛ inch or less) with a very sharp knife.

2. In a wide saucepan combine the water and caster sugar then bring to the boil to dissolve the sugar. Add the orange slices and simmer over a very low heat until translucent (about 60 minutes). Remove from the heat and leave to stand overnight.

To make the pastry:

3. Place the flour and margarine in a bowl and using your fingertips, combine the mixture until it resembles fine breadcrumbs.

4. Make a well in the mixture and add the icing sugar. Add sufficient water to dissolve the sugar, then combine with the flour mix to form a dough.

5. Chill for 20 minutes then roll out on a lightly-floured surface to line a 22.5cm/9 inch flan tin. Cover the pastry with foil and fill with baking beans, place in the pre-heated oven and bake for 10 to 15 minutes. Remove the beans and foil and return to the oven for a further 5 minutes. Remove from the oven and leave to cool.

To make the filling:

6. Melt the chocolate in a bowl over a pan of hot water then coat the flan base and sides using a pastry brush.

7. Mix 30ml/2tbsp of soya milk with the custard powder until smooth, then pour this into a pan with the remaining milk, orange juice and agar flakes. Bring to the boil, stirring constantly.

8. When the liquid has thickened, add the sugar and margarine and whisk until smooth. Allow to cool then place in the flan case and smooth. Chill.

To decorate:

9. If possible, complete this stage just before serving. Remove the orange slices from the syrup and drain well. Cut half of the slices in half, and the remaining slices into quarters.

10. Arrange a row of quarter slices along the outer edge of the tart, on top of the custard, with the rounded edges of the slices pointed outwards. Then place a row of overlapping half slices so that they just overlap the top of the first row. Continue with this pattern, alternating rows, until you reach the centre. The top should now resemble the petals of a flower.

11. Heat the apricot jam gently until it melts then brush it over the oranges to glaze.

Brandy Snap Fruit Baskets
can be vegan

Do try making these baskets - it's easier than you might think.

Makes 12

50g/2oz vegan margarine
50g/2oz sugar
50g/2oz golden syrup
50g/2oz plain flour
5ml/1tsp ground cinnamon
½ lemon, grated rind only
150ml/5fl oz double cream (or almond cream for a vegan version)
1 kiwi, peeled, sliced and each piece quartered
100g/4oz black grapes, halved and seeded
100g/4oz green grapes, halved and seeded
100g/4oz pineapple pieces
100g/4oz strawberries, quartered
1 mango, peeled and diced
fresh mint sprigs

Pre-heat the oven to 180°C, 350°F or Gas Mark 4

1. Grease 2 baking sheets. Have 2 small bowls or scrubbed oranges ready to shape the baskets. Mix together all the prepared fruit.

2. Put the margarine, sugar and golden syrup into a saucepan and heat gently, stirring until the sugar has dissolved and the margarine melted. Do not allow to boil. Remove from the heat. Stir in the flour, cinnamon and grated lemon rind with a wooden spoon until well mixed.

3. Place the mixture on a baking tray, 2 teaspoons at a time and about 4 inches apart to allow it to spread. Cook for about 8 minutes, until golden. Remove from the oven and leave for about 30 seconds. Lift off with a palette knife and shape over an orange or bowl to shape the baskets. Repeat to make 12 baskets.

4. Allow to cool. Spoon in a little double cream or almond cream. Fill with the mixed fruit and decorate with the mint leaves.

Fig and Banana Pudding
vegan

An old Italian proverb urges us to peel a fig for a friend and a peach for an enemy – this dessert is certainly a wonderful way to end a meal with friends.

400g/14oz ready-to-eat figs
1 banana, sliced
50g/2oz brown sugar
100g/4oz breadcrumbs
1 orange, juice and rind
50g/2oz vegan margarine, melted
5-10ml/1-2tsp brandy
25g/1oz pecan nuts, chopped finely

Pre-heat the oven to 190°C, 375°F or Gas Mark 5

1. Place the figs in a small amount of water, cover and simmer until they have softened. Drain and put on one side.

2. In an ovenproof dish, layer the figs, banana, sugar and breadcrumbs, orange rind, melted margarine, orange juice and brandy, finishing with a layer of breadcrumbs and sugar. Sprinkle with the nuts.

3. Place in the centre of the oven and bake for about 30 to 35 minutes until the topping is golden and crunchy.

Sweet Plum Dumplings

These dumplings are delicious served with a sharp fruit purée or
vanilla custard.

4 medium-sized potatoes
I free-range egg
100-150g/4-5oz wholegrain flour (depending on potatoes)
225g/8oz fresh plums
30ml/2tbsp raw cane sugar
pinch cinnamon
100g/4oz breadcrumbs
50g/2oz raw cane sugar

1. Bake the potatoes in their jackets then leave to cool.

2. Skin the potatoes and mash until very smooth.

3. Beat in the egg, then add sufficient flour to form a dough.
   This should be done with as little flour as possible. Leave to
   rest in the refrigerator for 90 minutes.

4. Take the stones out of the plums by cutting in half.

5. Roll out the dough to 1cm/½ inch thickness and cut rounds
   with a 7cm/3 inch cutter. Place half a plum in each circle.
   Fill the cavity with the mixed sugar and cinnamon. Fold the
   dough into the centre and form into a ball.

6. Bring plenty of salted water to the boil in a deep saucepan,
   carefully place the dumplings in the water and simmer for 3
   to 4 minutes. Remove the dumplings and drain.

7. Heat a little oil in a deep frying pan. Add the breadcrumbs
   and sugar and fry to a golden brown. Add the dumplings,
   roll in the breadcrumb mixture and serve.

*Almost any fruit or jam can be used as a filling. For added
flavour, chopped nuts or spices can be used in the breadcrumb
and sugar mixture.*

Sweet Potato and Banana Pudding
vegan

This may sound an unusual dessert, but it truly is delicious, and completely dairy-free. It has a taste and texture reminiscent of bread pudding, with a Caribbean twist.

4 medium-sized sweet potatoes
2 bananas
50g/2oz vegan margarine
2.5ml /½tsp cinnamon
2.5ml/½tsp nutmeg
50g/2oz brown sugar
150ml/5fl oz soya milk
75g/3oz raisins
50g/2oz pine nuts, toasted
15ml/1tbsp brown sugar

Pre-heat the oven to 180°C, 350°F or Gas Mark 4

1. Bake the potatoes until cooked then remove from the oven and leave to cool.

2. In a blender, liquidize the potato, banana, margarine, cinnamon, nutmeg, sugar and soya milk until smooth.

3. Place in an ovenproof dish and cover with the raisins and pine nuts. Sprinkle with the sugar and place in the oven for about 15 minutes.

Banana and Coconut Iced Dessert
vegan

A delicious combination of flavours – this recipe is a great favourite with adults and children alike, particularly when served with a chocolate sauce!

100g /4oz sugar
300ml/10fl oz water
3 bananas
75g/3oz creamed coconut, roughly chopped
150ml/5fl oz orange juice
15ml/1tbsp lemon juice
To garnish: 30ml/2tbsp desiccated coconut, toasted
mint sprigs

1. Put the sugar and water into a medium-sized saucepan and heat gently until the sugar dissolves. Bring to the boil and simmer for a couple of minutes, then remove from the heat and cool slightly.

2. Meanwhile place the bananas, creamed coconut and juices into a food processor and blend until smooth.

3. Add this mixture to the sugar syrup and stir.

4. Pour the mixture into a freezer-safe container and place in the freezer until half-frozen. Mash the mixture well, breaking up any ice particles, and return to the freezer until solid.

5. Remove from the freezer 20 minutes before serving, mash with a fork to break up and shape with spoons or an ice cream scoop. Decorate with mint sprigs and toasted desiccated coconut.

50g/2oz chopped pistachio nuts can be added to the mixture before freezing.

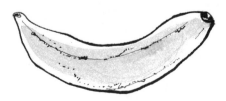

Caramelized Cider Apples
can be vegan

A great dessert to have for Hallowe'en supper.

4 large Bramley apples
the juice of half a lemon
30ml/2tbsp currants
25g/1oz roast hazelnuts, chopped
50g/2oz butter or vegan margarine, softened
210ml/7fl oz sweet vegan cider
175g/6oz white sugar

Pre-heat the oven to 220°C, 425°F or Gas Mark 7

1. Grease a baking dish to hold the apples. Peel the apples and brush with lemon juice. Remove the cores and place in the baking dish.

2. Mix the currants, hazelnuts and softened butter or margarine together. Fill each apple centre with the mixture.

3. Pour the cider into the dish and place a small piece of foil on the top of each apple. Cook in the oven for 30 to 40 minutes until the apples are tender, basting them frequently during cooking. Remove the foil for the last 5 minutes.

4. When the apples are cooked, turn off the oven and leave while preparing the caramel. Put the sugar and 45ml/3tbsp of water in a saucepan over a medium heat. Cook until a golden syrup has formed, being careful not to burn. Pour over the apples and serve immediately with cream or a soya cream alternative.

Pear Bread Pudding
can be vegan

Bread pudding is always popular, but this recipe transforms it into a
flavoursome, sophisticated dessert.

Serves 6

100g/4oz currant or sultanas
30ml/2tbsp calvados or brandy
125g/5oz butter or vegan margarine, softened
150g/6oz soft brown sugar
5ml/1tsp ground cinnamon
1 lemon, zest only
50g/2oz chopped almonds
200g/7oz stale bread
600g/1lb 5oz pears
30ml/2tbsp brown sugar
To garnish: toasted flaked almonds

Pre-heat the oven to 200°C, 400°F or Gas Mark 6

1. Soak the currants or sultanas in calvados or brandy.

2. Generously grease a 20cm (8 inch) ovenproof dish or 6
   individual ramekins using 25g/1oz of the butter or margarine.

3. Put the remaining 100g/4oz of butter or margarine in a bowl
   with the sugar and cream together well. Stir in the
   cinnamon, lemon zest, almonds and currants or sultanas.

4. Use a processor to turn the bread into breadcrumbs then stir
   these into the mixture.

5. Peel and core the pears and slice thinly.

6. Arrange one third of the breadcrumb mixture in the bottom
   of the ovenproof dish. Place half the pears on top, then
   another layer of bread. Add the rest of the pears and top
   with the remaining bread mixture.

7. Sprinkle with the 2 tablespoons of sugar, cover with foil and
   bake for 50 minutes. Remove the foil for the last 10 minutes

of cooking to brown the top. (If using individual ramekins, cover with foil and bake for 40 minutes, then remove the foil and brown for a further 5 to 10 minutes.)

8. Scatter the top with toasted almonds and serve with cream or soya cream alternative.

This is a particularly versatile recipe as the nuts, dried fruit and spirits can all be varied.

Crème Pâtissière
vegan

A delicious alternative to the classic French recipe.

300ml/10fl oz soya milk
1 vanilla pod
30ml/2tbsp custard powder
30ml/2tbsp caster sugar
2.5ml/½tsp vanilla essence
120ml/4fl oz soya cream

1. Heat the soya milk to boiling point. Add a vanilla pod, turn off the heat and leave to stand for 30 minutes.

2. Place the custard powder and caster sugar in a bowl. Mix to a smooth paste with a little of the soya milk.

3. Remove the vanilla pod from the remaining milk, add the custard paste and mix well.

4. Bring to the boil, stirring continually. Reduce the heat to a simmer and cook for a further 2 minutes.

5. Remove from the heat and stir in the vanilla essence and the soya cream. Allow to cool completely before using.

Try adding different flavourings to the crème – the zest of half an orange or a tangerine is traditional, but try chocolate.

Orange Tapioca Pudding
vegan

This is an aromatic Indian-style pudding but with a definite French influence
– a winning combination.

2 large oranges
600ml/1 pint sweetened soya milk
50g/2oz tapioca
75g/3oz desiccated coconut
pinch of allspice
150ml/5fl oz soya cream
25g/1oz caster sugar
10ml/2tsp brandy
20ml/4tsp orange flower water

1. Add the zest of the oranges to the milk and simmer gently for 20 minutes.

2. Add the tapioca, 50g of the coconut and the allspice to the milk and bring to the boil. Simmer gently for 15 minutes, stirring occasionally, until the pudding thickens.

3. Meanwhile, toast the remaining coconut and set aside. Chop the orange flesh and mix with the soya cream.

4. Add the soya cream and orange flesh mixture to the tapioca, along with the sugar, brandy and orange flower water. Stir, transfer to serving dishes and top with the remaining coconut.

Lemon and Lime Pond Pudding
can be vegan

A rich but surprisingly refreshing dessert.

225g/8oz self-raising flour
a pinch of salt
100g/4oz vegetarian suet
120ml/4fl oz iced water
100g/4oz butter or vegan margarine, diced
1 medium lemon
half a lime, sliced
100g/4oz raw cane sugar

1. Sift the flour and salt into a bowl. Add the suet and mix lightly with a fork. Make a well in the centre of the flour and add the water, a little at a time. Mix with a knife to make a soft dough.

2. Turn the dough out on to a floured surface and knead until it is free of cracks. Roll it out to a thickness of 7mm/¼ inch.

3. Cut a quarter of the dough and set aside for the lid. With the remaining dough, line a well-greased 600ml/1 pint heatproof pudding basin.

4. Put half the butter or margarine in the bottom of the basin. Prick the lemon all over with a skewer and sit it upright in the butter, arrange the lime slices around the lemon. Cover with the sugar and remaining butter.

5. Roll out the remaining dough for a lid. Dampen the edges and press it into place.

6. Cover the basin firstly with a layer of greaseproof paper, overlapping the sides of the basin, and then with foil. Tie on tightly with string.

7. Stand the basin in a large saucepan and pour in sufficient boiling water to reach three-quarters up the basin. Boil for 2 hours – keep topping up with boiling water so it doesn't boil dry.

8. To serve, remove the foil and paper and cut into the pudding with a sharp knife. It will reveal a wonderful pond of buttery syrup. Serve immediately.

Black Cherry and Kirsch Truffle Desserts

vegan

The classic combination of cherries, dark chocolate and nuts in this dairy-free recipe is simply wonderful.

Serves 8

350g/12 oz black cherries, stoned and chopped, canned can be used
60ml/4tbsp kirsch liqueur
5ml/1tsp almond essence
200g/7oz vegan dark chocolate
175g/6oz creamed coconut, roughly chopped or grated
100g/4oz hard (block) vegan margarine
200g/7oz vegan almond crunch biscuits
50g/2oz hazelnuts, roughly chopped

1. Lightly oil 8 ramekin dishes with a neutral oil and line with silicone baking parchment.

2. Place the fresh or canned cherries in a bowl and pour over the kirsch liqueur and almond essence. Leave to marinate for 2 hours.

3. Melt the chocolate, creamed coconut and vegan margarine together over a gentle heat.

4. Roughly crush the almond crunch biscuits and stir into the melted mixture with the hazelnuts. Add the marinated fruit and any remaining liquid.

5. Pour the mixture into the prepared ramekin dishes and lightly smooth the top. Cover and chill for 2 hours.

6. Turn out the desserts and serve on individual plates.

Chocolate, Raisin and Amaretto Ice Cream
vegan

No dairy ingredients, but the combination of rich flavour and creamy texture will make this a favourite.

Serves 4 to 6

50g/2oz raisins
22.5ml/1 1/2tbsp amaretto syrup
22.5ml/1 1/2tbsp maple syrup
450ml/15fl oz soya milk
100ml/7tbsp sunflower oil
10ml/2tsp vanilla essence
100g/4oz vegan dark chocolate, coarsely grated

1. Place the raisins in a small bowl and pour over the amaretto liqueur. Leave to soak until most of the liqueur has been absorbed.

2. Pour 300ml/10fl oz of the soya milk into ice cube trays and place in the freezer or freezer compartment of your refrigerator for about 4 or 5 hours or until frozen solid.

3. Put the remaining soya milk and the remaining ingredients except the grated chocolate in a blender. Add the now-frozen soya milk cubes and blend until completely smooth. Stir in the coarsely grated chocolate.

4. The ice cream can be served immediately, or returned to the freezer if a firmer ice cream is desired. Remember to allow the ice cream to defrost for about 40 minutes, or until the preferred consistency is achieved, before serving.

Rum and Raisin Tart
vegan

This unusual tart has a light, crisp coconut pastry which beautifully complements the creamed coconut and almond filling. The addition of rum-soaked raisins completes this vegan dessert!

For the pastry:

175g/6oz unbleached flour
25g/1oz desiccated coconut
25g/1oz icing sugar
75g/3oz vegan margarine
45-60ml/3-4tbsp soya milk

For the filling:

75g/3oz raisins
45-60ml/3-4tbsp rum
100g/4oz creamed coconut, chopped
300ml/10fl oz soya milk (or a combination of soya milk and soya cream)
75g/3oz ground almonds
50g/2oz soft brown sugar

Pre-heat the oven to 220°C, 425°F or Gas Mark 7

1. Soak the raisins in the rum for 1 hour.

2. To make the pastry, place the flour, desiccated coconut and icing sugar in a large mixing bowl, rub in the margarine until the mixture resembles bread crumbs. Add enough soya milk to form a smooth dough. Cover with cling film and place in the refrigerator for 30 minutes.

3. Roll out the pastry and line a greased 23cm/9 inch loose-bottomed flan tin, prick the base with a fork and bake for 10 minutes. Take the pastry case out of the oven, then reduce the oven temperature to 190°C, 375°F or Gas Mark 5.

4. To make the filling, heat the coconut cream and soya milk gently in a saucepan until the coconut has dissolved. Add the ground almonds and brown sugar and stir until combined.

5. Add the raisins and any remaining rum to the creamed coconut mixture. Pour the filling into the part cooked pastry case and bake for 25 to 30 minutes. Dust with icing sugar mixed with equal quantities of toasted desiccated coconut for a really special finish to the tart.

This dessert becomes firmer as it cools, and is best served warm.

Baked Apricots
vegan

A delightful way to use luscious fresh apricots when in season. Chocolate ice cream may not seem an obvious combination but makes a rich and interesting contrast to the fresh fruit.

900g/2lb fresh apricots
45ml/3tbsp demerara sugar
1 vanilla pod, broken
45ml/3tbsp peach liqueur
45ml/3tbsp water
50g/2oz pecan nuts, chopped finely

Pre-heat the oven to 180°C, 350°F or Gas Mark 4

1. Wash and wipe the apricots and make an incision on the top of each one with a sharp knife.

2. Place in an ovenproof dish, sprinkle with the sugar and add the vanilla pod.

3. Pour over the liqueur and water and bake uncovered until the apricots are soft, about 45 minutes.

4. Remove from the oven, sprinkle with the pecan nuts and serve immediately with chocolate ice cream.

Fruit Brulée
vegan

A simple dessert for a summer dinner party.

350g/12oz mixed summer fruits
60ml/4tbsp brandy
200ml/71/2fl oz carton soya cream
225g/8oz soya yoghurt, plain
8 drops vanilla essence
65g/2.5oz demerara sugar

1. Place the fruits in 4 flameproof dishes. Pour one tablespoon of brandy over each dish.

2. Mix the soya cream and yoghurt together and add the vanilla essence.

3. Spread the yoghurt mixture over the fruit and chill for 2 hours.

4. Sprinkle the sugar over the dishes and place them under a very hot grill until the sugar caramelises. Serve immediately.

Cashew Nut Cream
vegan

A wonderful dairy-free alternative to serve with desserts or fruit.

100g/4oz cashew nuts
150ml/5fl oz water
maple syrup to taste

1. Grind the cashew nuts until fine.

2. Put the water into a liquidizer, sprinkle the nuts on top and blend until smooth. Sweeten to taste with the maple syrup.

Miscellaneous

Autumn Quinoa Bread
can be vegan

This original recipe makes twenty-four dinner rolls
or two 900g/2lb loaf tins.

40g/1 ½oz fresh yeast
250ml/9fl oz warm water (blood-heat)
pinch of sugar
225ml/8fl oz warm buttermilk (blood-heat) *– use water for a vegan recipe*
50ml/2fl oz honey *– use molasses or maple syrup for a vegan recipe*
75ml/5tbsp corn oil
120ml/4fl oz pumpkin purée – instructions below
15ml/1tbsp salt
225ml/8fl oz cornmeal
225ml/8fl oz cooked Quinoa – instructions below
6 cups (approx) unbleached white flour
toasted pumpkin seeds to decorate (optional)

Pre-heat the oven to 190°C, 375°F or Gas Mark 5
when you have put the dough to prove

1. Place the yeast in a small bowl with the warm water and a pinch of sugar. Leave in a warm place for a few minutes to check that it is beginning to work.

2. In a large bowl combine the warm buttermilk, honey, oil, pumpkin purée (see below), salt, cornmeal and cooked Quinoa (see below). Beat with a whisk until smooth. Add the yeast mixture and beat for a further minute. Add the unbleached flour half a cup at a time, beating as you add it. You are aiming for a soft dough which just clears the sides of the bowl. The amount of flour this takes will vary according to the flour used and other invisible factors! So use your own judgement.

3. Tip the dough out onto a lightly-floured surface and knead for about three minutes. The dough should become smooth and springy to the touch. Place in a large, clean, oiled bowl, turning once to cover the upper surface of the dough with oil. Cover with cling film and leave in a warm place until doubled in size. This takes about thirty minutes in my kitchen because it is very warm. So, again, use your own judgement. It could take up to two hours!

4. Punch the dough down in the bowl and once more turn out onto a floured surface. Cut into two for large loaves, knead

lightly, shape and put into greased tins. I use white vegetable fat for this as it does not get absorbed into the loaf so easily as oil, so the loaf is less likely to stick in the tin. If making dinner rolls, then cut into 24 pieces and shape as you like. Place on greased baking sheets with space to expand. Cover loaves or rolls loosely with cling film and leave to prove until doubled in size – approximately 20 minutes.

5. Turn on the oven when you have put the dough to prove. When the dough has proved, glaze with egg or dust with cornmeal. With a serrated knife, make ¼ inch deep cuts in the surface. Decorate – I put toasted pumpkin seeds on top.

6. Bake in the pre-heated oven, loaves for 40 to 45 minutes, rolls for 15 to 20 minutes. Check halfway through the cooking time and turn if necessary to ensure even cooking. Remove from the oven and immediately place on cooling racks. Enjoy!

Pumpkin Purée

Pre-heat the oven to 180°C, 350°F or Gas Mark 4

1. Cut off the top of the pumpkin and scoop out the fibre and seeds – instructions for toasting below. Cut the pumpkin into large cubes, leaving the skin on.

2. Place flesh down in a baking dish filled with water to a depth of one inch. Cover and bake in a heated oven for 1 to 1½ hours, until tender. Remove from the oven and cool to room temperature.

3. Peel off the skin and discard. Purée the pulp until smooth. The easiest way to do this is in a food processor, with a metal blade. Cover the purée and keep in the fridge for up to five days, or freeze for nine months.

4. You can wash the seeds, separate them from the fibre and toast in the oven on an oiled tray. This takes 10 to 15 minutes. Check every few minutes, stirring the seeds to ensure even cooking. They are done when they are golden brown and smell of nuts. Sprinkle the seeds on top of the bread after glazing, before cooking.

Cooked Quinoa

Measure one cup of Quinoa. Rinse well. Add two cups of water. Bring to the boil, cover and simmer over a low heat until all water has been absorbed and the grain is soft (about 10 to 15 minutes). Leave to cool.

Spiced Almond Dip
vegan

A Cordon Vert classic – serve as a dip, a dressing, or spread on bruschertta or crostini bases – this one is always a winner.

40g/1 ½oz blanched, flaked almonds
1 clove garlic, crushed
a pinch of cayenne pepper
2.5ml/½tsp salt
2 small tomatoes, skinned and finely chopped
30-45ml/2-3tbsp red wine vinegar
150-200ml/5fl oz olive or almond oil
crudités to serve

1. Lightly roast the almonds and allow to cool completely.

2. Grind the almonds finely (e.g. in a nut grinder).

3. Place the ground almonds in a liquidizer with the garlic, cayenne, salt, tomatoes and vinegar. Blend well.

4. While the blender is still operating, add the oil very slowly until amalgamated.

5. Chill well and serve with crudités or as a salad dressing.

Spicy Sweetcorn Fritters
can be vegan

Deceptively simple, these fritters have an exotic spicy flavour and are delicious served with a satay (peanut) sauce.

350g/12oz frozen sweetcorn kernels
90ml/6tbsp wholemeal flour
90ml/6tbsp rice flour
10ml/2tsp sugar
20ml/4tsp vegetarian red curry paste
15ml/1tbsp shoyu
5ml/1tsp lime zest
groundnut oil to deep fry

1. Place the sweetcorn, flour, rice flour and sugar in a bowl and gradually work in the red curry paste, soy sauce and lime zest to form a dough. Use extra rice flour if the dough is too sticky.

2. Form into small, flat cakes about 4cm/1½ inches across.

3. Heat 10cm/4 inches of oil in a deep pan and fry the cakes in batches for 3 to 4 minutes, until crisp and golden. Drain on kitchen paper and serve with dipping sauces.

Tirvash: Mixed Grilled Vegetable Pickle
vegan

A flavoursome middle Eastern dish.

1 large red pepper
1 large yellow or orange pepper
30ml/2tbsp olive oil
1 large courgette, diced
10 green olives
10 black olives
20ml/4tsp capers
4 large Turkish pickled peppers
2 large plum tomatoes
10ml/2tsp chopped mint
120ml/4fl oz sweet vinegar
5ml/1tsp sugar
5ml/1tsp tomato purée

1. Grill the peppers until very black and blistered.
2. Peel the skin and cut into strips (saving as much of the juices as possible).
3. Heat the olive oil.
4. Sauté the courgette until golden brown.
5. Add the other solid ingredients and mix thoroughly.
6. Finally, add the vinegar, sugar and tomato purée and stir.
7. Serve with hot pitta bread and cheese.

Parkdale, home to the Vegetarian Society

Cordon Vert graduates

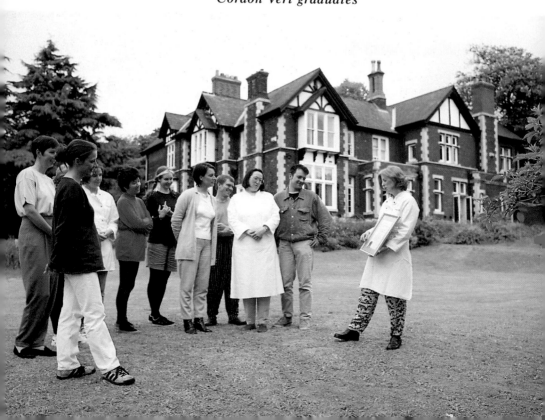

Above: Lyn Weller, tutor at the Cordon Vert Cookery School
Below: tool selection and techniques are taught to Cordon Vert students

Pasta making session

Barbecue Tomato Sauce
vegan

This recipe makes about a pint of sauce. It's very easy to make and full of flavour – don't wait for a summer barbecue to use it.

15ml/1tbsp olive oil
1 medium onion, peeled and finely chopped
1 clove garlic, crushed
2 stalks celery, finely chopped
400g/14oz tin chopped tomatoes
15ml/1tbsp tomato purée
1 thin slice of lemon
30ml/2tbsp white wine vinegar
225ml/8fl oz apple juice (dilute apple juice concentrate by 1:7)
2 bay leaves
shoyu or tamari, to taste
freshly ground black pepper

1. Heat the oil and gently fry the onion, garlic and celery until softened but not browned.
2. Add the chopped tomatoes, tomato purée, lemon slice, vinegar, apple juice and bay leaves.
3. Bring to the boil, then simmer uncovered for 25 minutes to reduce the sauce.
4. Allow to cool. Remove the bay leaves, but leave the lemon slice in.
5. Blend until smooth. Season to taste with shoyu or tamari and black pepper.
6. Reheat to serve.

A little arrowroot can be used to thicken the sauce slightly and prevent 'bleeding' if the sauce is to be served plated.

Rhubarb and Apple Chutney
vegan

A good friend of mine, Ros, is a connoisseur of chutneys and claims that this is one of the best she's tasted. It is a fabulous recipe to make use of the abundance of rhubarb in the garden – this recipe makes about one and a half kilos (3lb) of really excellent chutney.

900g/2lb rhubarb, chopped into 2.5cm/1 inch pieces
225g/8oz cooking apples, peeled, cored and quartered
225g/8oz onions, chopped finely
15g/½oz freshly grated ginger
5ml/1 tsp salt
5ml/1 tsp good curry powder
450ml/15fl oz ready-spiced pickling vinegar
450g/1lb sugar

1. Have a selection of clean, dry jars with lids at the ready – warm the jars in a moderate oven for 5 minutes immediately before adding the chutney.

2. Place the rhubarb, apple and onion in a large saucepan with 15ml/1tbsp of water and simmer, covered, until cooked.

3. Add the ginger, salt and curry powder and half the required vinegar to the rhubarb mixture and cook for about 40 minutes.

4. Dissolve the sugar in the remaining vinegar and add to the pan. Simmer very slowly until the consistency has thickened, there should be no unabsorbed liquid.

5. Fill the prepared jars and cover.

Chestnut and Feta Balls

Surprise your guests with the unusual combination of chestnuts and feta
cheese – they complement each other perfectly.

100g/4oz dried chestnuts or 225g/8oz cooked weight
75g/3oz onion, very finely diced
15ml/1tbsp fresh coriander, finely chopped
3ml/½tsp dried sage
50g/2oz vegetarian feta cheese, crumbled
2 free-range eggs
5ml/1tsp ground cumin
unbleached white flour
olive oil for frying
salt and freshly ground black pepper

1. Soak the dried chestnuts for 6 hours, drain and cook in fresh
   water for 40 minutes, or until soft. Drain again and then
   mash the chestnuts in a bowl.

2. Add the rest of the ingredients except the flour and oil and
   season to taste.

3. Shape the mixture into walnut-sized balls and dust with
   flour to prevent sticking.

4. Heat the oil in a frying pan and fry the balls until they are
   golden and crisp on the outside.

5. Serve hot or cold, garnished with lemon wedges.

Almond, Orange and Ginger Biscotti

A variation on a traditional Italian biscuit. Don't be alarmed – they are supposed to be hard. Dunk into a glass of sweet white wine to enjoy them at their best.

225g/8oz plain flour
175g/6oz caster sugar
pinch of salt
2.5ml/½tsp baking powder
2 free-range eggs, beaten
75ml/5tbsp stem ginger, roughly chopped
10ml/2tsp orange juice
1 orange, grated rind only
100g/4oz whole almonds, toasted and roughly chopped

Pre-heat the oven to 200°C, 400°F or Gas Mark 6

1. Sift the flour, sugar, salt and baking powder into a bowl and beat in the eggs chopped ginger and orange juice.

2. Stir in the rind and nuts, then work all the ingredients together until you have a soft dough. If it is sticky at this stage, add a little more flour.

3. Turn the dough onto a floured work surface and knead until smooth, again sprinkling with flour if it is too sticky.

4. Divide the dough into four and form into rolls about 10cm/4 inches long. Place these on two greased baking sheets and bake for about 30 minutes, until golden brown.

5. Remove from the oven and slice diagonally into 1cm/½ inch thick slices. Arrange on a baking sheet and bake for a further 10 minutes.

6. When cooked, transfer the biscotti to a wire rack to cool.

These biscuits will keep for 7 days in an airtight container

Pancakes
vegan

These pancakes can be filled with a sweet or savoury filling – try ratatouille, Chinese or curried vegetables or a hot fruit filling.

Makes 8 pancakes

225g/8oz gram flour
5ml/1tsp salt
2.5ml/½tsp bicarbonate of soda
400ml/14fl oz water
30ml/2tbsp fresh coriander, chopped
15ml/1tbsp groundnut oil

1. Sift the flour into a large bowl and stir in the salt and bicarbonate of soda. Add the water gradually, beating well until a smooth batter is obtained.

2. Stir in the coriander and leave to stand for 20 minutes.

3. Heat a little oil in a non-stick frying pan, and add enough batter to just cover the base of the pan.

4. Cook for about one minute then flip over and cook for a further minute. Remove from the pan and keep warm.

5. Repeat until all the batter has been used.

Layer the pancakes with greaseproof paper and keep them warm on a plate over a pan of simmering water.

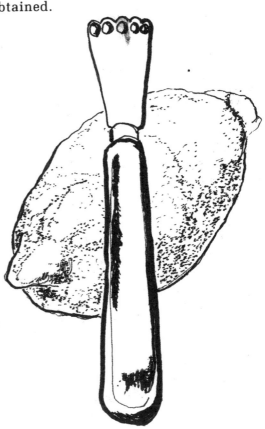

Tuscan Olive Bread
can be vegan

A recipe to transport you to the Italian sunshine – the flavours are strong and delicious.

For the bread:

900g/2lb strong plain flour
25g/1oz dried yeast
60ml/2fl oz olive oil
150ml/5fl oz lukewarm water
2 sun-dried tomatoes, finely chopped
1 sprig fresh rosemary
a pinch of salt

For the topping:

15ml/1 tbsp oil
1 red onion, finely chopped
3 cloves garlic, crushed
6 fresh plum tomatoes, chopped
a dash of red wine
50g/2oz feta cheese, crumbled (omit for vegans)
25g/1oz black olives, pitted and halved
25g/1oz capers
salt and freshly ground black pepper

Pre-heat the oven to 220°C, 425°F or Gas Mark 7

To make the bread:

1. Mix all the ingredients in a large bowl, then knead and leave in a warm place to rise for 1 hour.

2. Briefly knead again and divide into 6 equal rounds.

3. Leave the dough to prove for a further 20 minutes then bake in the oven for about 15 minutes.

4. Remove from the oven, brush with olive oil and leave to cool.

To prepare the topping:

5. Heat the oil and fry the onions and garlic until soft.

6. Add the tomatoes, wine and seasoning and simmer until the sauce has reduced and is a paste-like consistency.

7. Stir in the cheese, olives and capers, and heat through gently.

8. Divide the mixture between the bases and serve at once.

Pumpkin Scones

An unusual and delicious variation on the popular teatime treat.

Makes 16

50g/2oz butter
25g/1oz raw brown sugar
1 free-range egg, beaten
400g/14oz pumpkin, cooked and mashed
25g/1oz prunes, pitted and chopped
225g/8oz self-raising flour, sifted
2.5ml/½tsp ground cinnamon

Pre-heat the oven to 220°C, 425°F or Gas Mark 7

1. Beat the butter and sugar until light and fluffy, add the egg and beat until combined.

2. Stir in the pumpkin, prunes, flour and cinnamon and mix to a soft dough.

3. Turn onto a floured surface and knead lightly until smooth.

4. Roll the dough out gently and evenly until about 2.5cm/1 inch thick. Cut into rounds using a 5cm/2 inch cutter.

5. Place on a lightly floured baking sheet and bake for about 20 minutes, until the scones are brown and sound hollow when tapped.

Index

More Books from . . .

We publish a wide range of books (currently over 200!), many for outdoor pursuits including walking, cycling, football & golf. We also publish excellent general interest books – and here is a selection:

Mildred Smith's Favourite Family Recipes

Published in association with **GRANADA TELEVISION**, this is the second cookery book from Mildred Smith – the much-loved traditional cookery star of Granada TV's "The Main Ingredient". In this, you'll find many famous traditional recipes for everything from a simple sauce through satisfying main courses to delicious desserts, including such tempting treats as sticky toffee pudding, banoffee pie and other sweets too nice to mention.   £6.95

Caravan and Holiday Cookery

You don't like take-away food, but you don't want to spend your entire holiday slaving over a hot stove. So how can you preserve your sanity and keep the family happy? Here's the answer – simple cookery using some ready-made items plus readily available fresh food. Over 100 tempting meals, none of which needs more than two rings and a grill. Lemon minted cod in 10 minutes – apple and coriander chicken in half an hour – oat crunch in no time at all. Why queue in a take-away?   £4.95

Exercises That Work For You: Non-strenuous fitness basics for body, mind and spirit

For many years, Elizabeth Graham Smith has run exercise and Tai Chi classes. In this book, she passes on her exercise programme for whole body and mind fitness. Her holistic message goes right through the book: fitness is a composite matter: tense muscles accompany tense minds and spirits; allow mind and spirit more freedom and some psychological hang-ups can vanish!   £6.95

FOR LOVERS OF THE GREAT OUTDOORS AND THE GREAT BRITISH TEA SHOP.
Tea Shop Walks are spreading faster than butter on a toasted teacake!

Walking really can be a pleasure with this wonderful series of walking books. Each book has 25 to 30 interesting and varied walks, with a tempting tea shop to enjoy either along the way or as a reward at the end of the walk. Titles in our *TEA SHOP WALKS* series include:

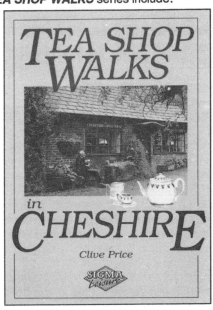

- ¤ *Tea Shop Walks in Cheshire*
- ¤ *Tea Shop Walks in The Chilterns*
- ¤ *Tea Shop Walks in Lancashire*
- ¤ *Tea Shop Walks in North Devon*
- ¤ *Tea Shop Walks in South Devon*
- ¤ *Tea Shop Walks in The Cotswolds*
- ¤ *Tea Shop Walks in The Lake District*
- ¤ *Tea Shop Walks in Cumbria*
- ¤ *Tea Shop Walks in The Peak District*
- ¤ *Tea Shop Walks in The Yorkshire Dales*
- ¤ *Tea Shop Walks in Staffordshire*
- ¤ *Tea Shop Walks in Shropshire*
- ¤ *Tea Shop Walks in Oxfordshire*
- ¤ *Tea Shop Walks in Surrey & Sussex*
- ¤ *Tea Shop Walks in Dorset & Wiltshire*
- ¤ *. . . with many more to come!*
- ¤ *Remember: only the Sigma Leisure series is RECOMMENDED BY THE TEA CLUB - the premier UK organisation for lovers of fine teas and afternoon tea establishments!*

All temptingly priced at £6.95!

Learn to Dance!

If you'd like to learn to dance but need to be shown the fundamentals – or if you want to brush up on what you learn at classes, these top-value packages are just what you need: Accurate and entertaining instructions plus professionally-performed music to match the dances!

COUNTRY & WESTERN LINE DANCING: for Cowgirls and Cowboys [book + cd package]

Judy Dygdon & Tony Conger

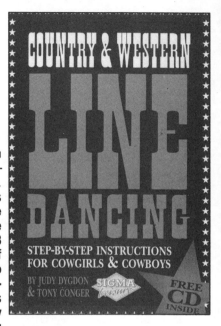

Here's the fastest-selling line-dance package in the UK! Line Dancing is sweeping the country – the hottest dance import since Rock 'n' Roll. Thousands enjoy it already and its popularity is still rocketing. Written by two American dance teachers, this was the first book & CD package published in Britain on the new dance craze – 53 accurately-described dances PLUS a CD of Country & Western music carefully chosen to match the dances. **This is the complete teach-yourself package.** Brimming with lively cartoons and anecdotes, it's the definitive guide to this new dance craze. And *all for £12.95* – less than you pay for most CDs!

NEW FOR 1998:

UK LINE DANCE FAVOURITES: step-by-step instructions

This is the companion volume to the above book by the same team of Judy Dygdon & Tony Conger. In this book, you'll find all the popular dances for UK linedancers – plus some more from 'over there' that will soon be popular 'over here'! 52 dances for £8.95 – great value! **Please note: separate CD available for this book.**

More to come! Look out for our CD guides to:

Salsa ~ Line Dancing ~ Modern Jive

FOOD FOR THOUGHT

The Vegetarian Society has campaigned for vegetarianism since 1847. An organisation with a central positive message, we are committed to safeguarding animal welfare, promoting a healthier diet and protecting the environment. With a staggering 5,000 people turning vegetarian in the UK each week, it is obvious that our message is getting through! As the leading authority on vegetarianism, the Society exists to promote vegetarianism in the UK and throughout the world through research, national campaigns, education, government lobbying, liaison with the food industry and via our cookery school.

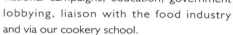
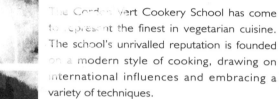

The Cordon Vert Cookery School has come to represent the finest in vegetarian cuisine. The school's unrivalled reputation is founded on a modern style of cooking, drawing on international influences and embracing a variety of techniques.

A highly qualified team of tutors provides inspirational courses to suit all levels of experience. A relaxed approach to practical tuition ensures an atmosphere in which individual talent and creativity can prosper. Cordon Vert students take with them a life–enhancing understanding of what vegetarian food is all about.

Joining The Vegetarian Society makes being a vegetarian easy. Members receive a full–colour quarterly magazine offering unique access to recipes, vegetarian news, new products, features, the vegetarian directory and a host of offers. A membership card entitles you to hundreds of discounts at restaurants and health food stores, while access to our members vegetarian hotline provides an exclusive information service. Our experts are only a phone call away!

We need your support if we are to continue operating at all levels to get the vegetarian message across. Initiatives such as *National Vegetarian Week* and campaigns against the exotic meat trade, battery farming and intensive fishing would not be possible without membership support. The Vegetarian Society is an independent voice, to let that voice be heard we need your support.

Join today and take your first step towards a healthier more ethical lifestyle. Call **0161 928 0793** for a free Starter Pack or details of The Cordon Vert Cookery School courses.

The Vegetarian Society Parkdale Dunham Road Altrincham Cheshire WA14 4QG
www.veg.org.uk Registered Charity No. 259358